SIMPLY
THE BEST
VEGETARIAN
BARBECUE
RECIPES

SIMPLY
THE BEST
VEGETARIAN
BARBECUE
RECIPES

WENDY HOBSON

EDITED BY CAROLYN HUMPHRIES

foulsham

LONDON • NEW YORK • TORONTO • SYDNEY

foulsham

The Publishing House, Bennetts Close,
Cippenham, Slough, Berkshire, SL1 5AP, England

ISBN 0-572-02418-5

Copyright © 1998 W. Foulsham & Co. Ltd.
Originally published under the title *Instant Vegetarian Barbecue Ideas*

Illustrations and cover artwork by Sophie Azimont

Printed in Great Britain by Cox & Wyman Ltd., Reading, Berks

CONTENTS

INTRODUCTION

There are so many vegetable variations you can enjoy on your barbecue, there's no need to be bored. Vegetables love the barbecue – and you'll love the treats you can create over the coals with these simple recipes. Mix and match, experiment to find the best combinations – there are plenty of options if you keep your eyes open for new vegetables on the supermarket or greengrocers' shelves and give them a try.

Unless you live in a place where the sunshine is guaranteed, you will want to take advantage of any good weather by having impromptu barbecues rather than planning them in advance and risking being drowned out! So lots of these ideas are simple and quick to prepare, but still give mouth-watering results.

Whether you are cooking an all-vegetarian barbecue, or making sure you have tasty vegetarian options for your family or guests, you can create colourful and interesting vegetable kebabs, tasty foil-wrapped parcels and vegetable burgers too. Go on – give it a try!

Notes on the Recipes

* The recipes use dairy products. For vegans, either omit the dairy products or use vegetarian alternatives. Make sure cheeses used are suitable for vegetarians too.

* A number of recipes use Worcestershire sauce. Traditional recipes include anchovies, so buy a vegetarian variety from health food shops.

* When following a recipe, use either metric, imperial or American measures; do not mix different sets of measurements.

* All spoon measurements are level: 1 tsp = 5 ml;
                                    1 tbsp = 15 ml.

* Eggs are medium unless otherwise stated.

* Use your favourite good-quality light oil, like sunflower or groundnut (peanut) oil, unless otherwise stated.

* All preparation and cooking times are approximate.

* Always wash and peel, if necessary, all fresh produce before use.

* Where fresh herbs are used, they are specified in the ingredients. You can substitute dried herbs as long as they have time to cook; never use them for sprinkling on finished dishes. If you use dried rather than fresh herbs, use no more than half the stated quantity as they are very pungent. Packets of frozen chopped herbs such as parsley and mint are much better than the dried varieties.

* Always pre-heat the barbecue for about 30 minutes before cooking (see page 13).

* Soak wooden skewers for about 1 hour before cooking to prevent charring.

BARBECUE BASICS

Here are some simple guidelines on getting the best out of your barbecue, and being ready for that quick and easy, inspirational meal!

Barbecuing is an easy technique which gives great results but it is not an exact science. You cannot really control the temperature of the charcoal; so you must control the distance you place the food from the heat – the nearer the food is to the heat, the higher the temperature and the faster the food will cook. Because the heat is direct, of course, the food cooks first on the outside, so you must allow the food enough time to cook right through. This means that larger pieces of food, such as large potatoes, need to be placed further from the coals, otherwise they will be charred on the outside before they are cooked inside. These principles apply whether you have a tiny Hibachi or a large gas-fired barbecue, and you will have to experiment and get to know your own equipment in order to get the best out of it.

On the whole, vegetables cook very quickly on the barbecue, so there is little waiting around. They do tend to dry out more than some other foods, however, so be redy with those tasty basting mixtures or flavoured oils to keep them moist and make sure you get delicious results.

Equipment

You can manage with your ordinary kitchen tools, of course, but if you are an enthusiast, it is a good idea to have a few long-handled utensils to make it easier when you are cooking on the barbecue. Have only what you need; more often than not, fancy gadgets are a waste of space. Your barbecue itself can be as small and simple or as impressive as you want – it doesn't make that much difference to the taste of the food!

Most people find briquettes of compressed charcoal are the easiest to use. They burn more slowly and at a higher temperature than lump charcoal, although this can light more quickly and so is useful for starting the barbecue.

If you really get hooked on the barbecue habit, you'll start to consider a bigger and better barbecue, perhaps with an electric or battery-operated spit and motor.

For the Fire

* Charcoal, firelighters, tapers, matches.
* Foil to line the barbecue (it makes it easier to clear up).
* Tongs for spreading the coals.
* Poker for flicking grey ash off the charcoal.
* Sprinkler bottle of water to douse flare-ups.
* Small shovel for adding coals and clearing ash afterwards.
* Bellows for encouraging the fire if it is dying down; blowing is hot and dirty work.
* Pile of sand for dousing the fire after cooking.
* Bucket of water, just in case.

* Cleaning materials; specialist ones are available from barbecue suppliers which you may find are more effective than ordinary kitchen cleansers.

For the Food

* Tongs and spatula with long wooden handles for turning foods.
* Basting brush with long wooden handle and a jug.
* Kebab skewers; always soak wooden skewers in cold water for at least 1 hour before use so that they do not char when cooking.
* Hinged wire grilles to hold soft food between layers of mesh so that it doesn't break up during cooking. They are ideal for fish, burgers or other similar foods.
* Knives, forks, chopping board.
* Foil for covering and wrapping food.
* Heat-resistant gloves and large apron.
* Trolley or small table for holding foods etc.

For the Guests

* Serving table.
* Crockery and cutlery, including serving cutlery.
* Drinks and glasses. Bottle and can openers, water jug, ice bucket.
* Tablecloth and sturdy napkins.

Safety

* Set up the barbecue on a stable, level surface in the open air, avoiding any overhanging trees or nearby low bushes.
* Light the fire carefully and make sure it is always attended.
* Never move a lighted barbecue.
* Never touch any part of the barbecue once it has been lit. Extremely hot charcoal will look white and powdery rather than glowing red.
* Avoid plastic- or metal-handled tools as they can melt or hold the heat.
* Douse flare-ups quickly.
* Dispose of ashes carefully when they are cold.
* Immerse burns immediately in cold water and keep under water until it feels cool. Cover with a dry, sterile dressing, if necessary, and seek medical attention if severe.

Lighting and Maintaining the Fire

* Tell your neighbours you are about to light a barbecue – especially if they have washing out!
* Line the barbecue with foil, shiny side up. Open the vents if the barbecue has them.
* Arrange a few pieces of broken firelighters in the base.
* Top with a few pieces of lump charcoal or wood chips.
* Arrange a few charcoal briquettes on top.
* Light the firelighters with a taper.

* When the charcoal has caught and is burning steadily, use long-handled tongs to spread the charcoal in a single layer and add more charcoal at the edges.

* Gradually add charcoal around the outside of the fire to keep it at a steady temperature; putting charcoal on top will smother it. Remember that the charcoal will maintain heat for some time, so don't add more coals if you are coming to the end of cooking.

* Douse the fire with sand when you have finished cooking and leave to cool completely.

Starting to Cook

* The fire should take about 30 minutes to reach cooking temperature, by which time the charcoal will be grey and powdery.

* Oil the rack lightly, then set it about 10 cm/4 in above the coals.

* The fire is ready if you can hold your hand at about that level for only 2–3 seconds.

* The centre of the charcoal will always be hotter than the edges, so you can use this to good effect when arranging your food on the rack. Allow plenty of space around the foods so that you can turn them easily and they are not too crowded to cook evenly.

* Plan your cooking order in advance so that you start with the foods with the longest cooking times.

* Remember that you can arrange your dessert foods on the barbecue and watch them cook while you are enjoying your main course.

Store-cupboard Stand-bys

If you like barbecuing, it makes sense to keep a few things handy in the cupboard or the freezer during the barbecue season so that you can create some interesting dishes at short notice. Start with some basics, and you'll soon learn the ingredients and seasonings you use most often.

* Spices such as cayenne, cinnamon, coriander (cilantro), cumin, nutmeg and ground or fresh minced ginger.

* Dried herbs such as bay leaves, oregano, rosemary, tarragon and thyme. Prepared frozen herbs are very good, especially mint and parsley.

* Sauces such as soy sauce, Tabasco sauce, tomato purée (paste), Worcestershire sauce, relishes and pickles.

* Seasonings and flavourings such as salt and pepper (of course!), capers, mustard, pesto sauce and sesame seeds.

* Vinegars such as white and red wine vinegar, balsamic vinegar and fruit vinegars.

* Lemon juice and other citrus juices.

* Olive or groundnut (peanut) oil and sesame oil.

* Garlic, onions and fresh root ginger.

* Honey, sugar, golden (light corn) syrup and treacle (molasses).

* Canned vegetables, pulses and vegetable mixtures such as lentils, tomatoes and ratatouille.

* Canned fruits such as passion fruit, peaches and lychees.

* Crackers and melba toast.

* French and other interesting continental breads in the freezer – par-baked loaves will give you that straight-from-the-oven smell!

MARINADES
AND SAUCES

If you have made a last-minute decision to have a
barbecue, a marinade can help you create a whole range
of different flavours with the simplest of ingredients.
Vegetables tend to absorb marinade flavours quickly, so
often just a short marinating time is all that is necessary
to create unusual dishes. If you have a little more time,
you can leave the vegetables to marinate for slightly
longer before barbecuing them to give even more
intense flavours.

~~~~~~~~~~~~~~~

White Wine Marinade

Use this marinade for firm vegetables such as cauliflower florets, onions, chicory (Belgian endive) or (bell) peppers.

Makes about 450 ml/ ¾ pt/2 cups

	METRIC	IMPERIAL	AMERICAN
Onion, chopped	1	1	1
Sprigs of parsley	2	2	2
Sprig of tarragon or thyme	1	1	1
Bay leaf	1	1	1
Dry white wine	300 ml	½ pt	1¼ cups
White wine vinegar or lemon juice	30 ml	2 tbsp	2 tbsp
Clear honey, warmed	10 ml	2 tsp	2 tsp
Oil	30 ml	2 tbsp	2 tbsp
Pinch of cayenne			
Salt and freshly ground black pepper			

1 Whisk together all the ingredients.

2 Marinate foods for at least 30 minutes.

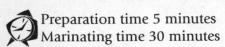 Preparation time 5 minutes
Marinating time 30 minutes

Red Wine Marinade

Prepare as for White Wine Marinade but substitute red wine for white and add a finely chopped garlic clove. Use for mushrooms, courgettes (zucchini), aubergines (eggplants), fennel, broccoli and root vegetables.

Oriental Marinade

This lighter marinade is ideal for vegetables such as carrots and mangetout (snow peas). Substitute 30 ml/2 tbsp of lemon juice if you do not have lime juice.

Makes about 450 ml/³/₄ pt/2 cups

	METRIC	IMPERIAL	AMERICAN
Lime juice	45 ml	3 tbsp	3 tbsp
Rice wine or white wine vinegar	45 ml	3 tbsp	3 tbsp
Light soy sauce	30 ml	2 tbsp	2 tbsp
Dry sherry	15 ml	1 tbsp	1 tbsp
Sesame oil	15 ml	1 tbsp	1 tbsp
Groundnut (peanut) oil	60 ml	4 tbsp	4 tbsp
Light brown sugar	15 ml	1 tbsp	1 tbsp
Chinese five-spice powder	2.5 ml	¹/₂ tsp	¹/₂ tsp
Large sprig of coriander (cilantro), chopped			

1 Mix together the lime juice, vinegar, soy sauce, sherry and sesame oil in a glass or ceramic bowl.

2 Gradually whisk in the groundnut oil, then stir in the remaining ingredients.

3 Marinate foods for at least 2 hours.

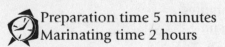
Preparation time 5 minutes
Marinating time 2 hours

Thai-style Marinade

Try this with mangetout (snow peas), courgettes (zucchini), root vegetables or mixed vegetable kebabs. Substitute 45 ml/ 3 tbsp of lemon juice if you do not have lime juice.

Makes about 450 ml/ ³/₄ pt/ 2 cups

	METRIC	IMPERIAL	AMERICAN
Lime juice	75 ml	5 tbsp	5 tbsp
Sesame oil	175 ml	6 fl oz	³/₄ cup
Garlic cloves, crushed	2–3	2–3	2–3
Roasted peanuts, crushed	45 ml	3 tbsp	3 tbsp
Light brown sugar	25 ml	1¹/₂ tbsp	1¹/₂ tbsp
Lemon grass stalk, chopped	1	1	1
Dried red chilli, crushed	2.5 ml	¹/₂ tsp	¹/₂ tsp
Chopped fresh coriander (cilantro)	45 ml	3 tbsp	3 tbsp
Vegetarian Worcestershire sauce	15 ml	1 tbsp	1 tbsp
Salt and freshly ground black pepper			

1 Whisk all the ingredients together in a glass or ceramic bowl and season generously with salt and pepper.

2 Marinate foods for at least 2 hours.

Preparation time 5 minutes
Marinating time 2 hours

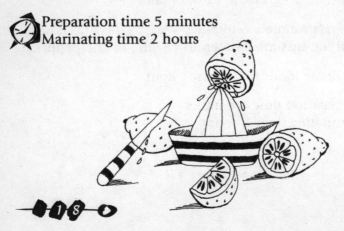

Sesame Lemon Marinade

This gives a tangy flavour to kebabs, especially those made with courgettes (zucchini).

Makes about 450 ml / ¾ pt / 2 cups

	METRIC	IMPERIAL	AMERICAN
Lemon juice	90 ml	6 tbsp	6 tbsp
Grated lemon rind	15 ml	1 tbsp	1 tbsp
Groundnut (peanut) oil	200 ml	7 fl oz	scant 1 cup
Sesame seeds	45 ml	3 tbsp	3 tbsp
Garlic cloves, crushed	2–3	2–3	2–3
Ground cumin	5 ml	1 tsp	1 tsp
Dried oregano	5 ml	1 tsp	1 tsp
Chopped fresh parsley	60 ml	4 tbsp	4 tbsp
Salt and freshly ground black pepper			

1 Mix together the lemon juice and rind. Gradually whisk in the oil.

2 Toast the sesame seeds in a dry pan until golden, then crush lightly.

3 Add all the remaining ingredients to the lemon juice and oil, seasoning generously with salt and pepper.

4 Marinate foods for at least 1 hour.

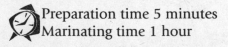
Preparation time 5 minutes
Marinating time 1 hour

Caribbean Marinade

Use this marinade for fruits or sweet vegetables.

Makes about 450 ml/³/₄ pt/2 cups

	METRIC	IMPERIAL	AMERICAN
Can of passion fruit or mango	400 g	14 oz	1 large
Orange juice	120 ml	4 fl oz	¹/₂ cup
Garlic cloves, crushed	3	3	3
Dark rum	30 ml	2 tbsp	2 tbsp
Black treacle (molasses)	30 ml	2 tbsp	2 tbsp
Lime juice	60 ml	4 tbsp	4 tbsp
Tabasco sauce	5 ml	1 tsp	1 tsp
Ground coriander (cilantro)	2.5 ml	¹/₂ tsp	¹/₂ tsp
Ground cumin	2.5 ml	¹/₂ tsp	¹/₂ tsp
Chopped fresh coriander (cilantro)	30 ml	2 tbsp	2 tbsp

1 Simmer the passion fruit with the orange juice in a small pan for 5 minutes, then rub through a sieve (strainer).

2 Mix with the remaining ingredients in a glass or ceramic bowl.

3 Marinate foods for at least 2 hours. Use any remaining marinade as a sauce.

Preparation time 10 minutes
Marinating time 2 hours

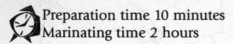

Garlic Marinade

Use this marinade for any vegetables.

Makes about 450 ml / ¾ pt / 2 cups

	METRIC	IMPERIAL	AMERICAN
Dry white wine	300 ml	½ pt	1¼ cups
Olive oil	120 ml	4 fl oz	½ cup
Bay leaf	1	1	1
Garlic cloves, crushed	2	2	2
Sugar	2.5 ml	½ tsp	½ tsp
Salt and freshly ground black pepper			

1 Whisk together all the ingredients.

2 Marinate foods for at least 30 minutes. Use any remaining marinade to baste foods while cooking.

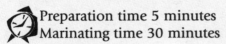 Preparation time 5 minutes
Marinating time 30 minutes

Rich Plum Sauce Marinade

This is ideal for vegetables such as (bell) peppers, onions or leeks. You can buy the plum sauce in supermarkets, or substitute a sweet relish.

Makes about 450 ml/¾ pt/2 cups

	METRIC	IMPERIAL	AMERICAN
Dry sherry	30 ml	2 tbsp	2 tbsp
Oriental plum sauce	150 ml	¼ pt	⅔ cup
Soy sauce	15 ml	1 tbsp	1 tbsp
Hoisin sauce	15 ml	1 tbsp	1 tbsp
Sesame oil	5 ml	1 tsp	1 tsp
Groundnut (peanut) oil	30 ml	2 tbsp	2 tbsp
Grated fresh root ginger	15 ml	1 tbsp	1 tbsp
Garlic cloves, crushed	2	2	2
Chopped fresh coriander (cilantro)	60 ml	4 tbsp	4 tbsp

1 Mix together the sherry, the plum, soy and hoisin sauces and the sesame oil.

2 Gradually whisk in the groundnut oil. Mix in the remaining ingredients.

3 Marinate foods for at least 3 hours.

Preparation time 5 minutes
Marinating time 3 hours

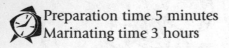

Quick Barbecue Sauce

Great served warm or cold with almost anything from the barbecue.

Makes about 300 ml / ½ pt / 1¼ cups

	METRIC	IMPERIAL	AMERICAN
Butter or margarine	50 g	2 oz	¼ cup
Onion, chopped	1	1	1
Tomato purée (paste)	5 ml	1 tsp	1 tsp
Red wine vinegar	30 ml	2 tbsp	2 tbsp
Light brown sugar	30 ml	2 tbsp	2 tbsp
Mustard powder	10 ml	2 tsp	2 tsp
Vegetarian Worcestershire sauce	30 ml	2 tbsp	2 tbsp
Water	150 ml	¼ pt	⅔ cup

1 Melt the butter or margarine and fry (sauté) the onion until soft.

2 Add the remaining ingredients, stirring together over a low heat until well blended. Bring to the boil, then simmer for 10 minutes.

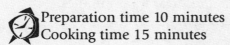

Preparation time 10 minutes
Cooking time 15 minutes

Indonesian Hot Peanut Sauce

This is best served warm with mixed vegetable kebabs or Quorn meals.

Makes about 450 ml / ¾ pt / 2 cups

	METRIC	IMPERIAL	AMERICAN
Water	120 ml	4 fl oz	½ cup
White wine vinegar	120 ml	4 fl oz	½ cup
Sugar	50 g	2 oz	¼ cup
Peanut butter	100 g	4 oz	½ cup
Grated fresh root ginger	30 ml	2 tbsp	2 tbsp
Garlic clove, crushed	1	1	1
Soy sauce	45 ml	3 tbsp	3 tbsp
Chopped fresh coriander (cilantro)	15 ml	1 tbsp	1 tbsp
Pinch of cayenne			
Salt			
Sesame oil	15 ml	1 tbsp	1 tbsp

1 Boil the water, vinegar and sugar for 5 minutes, stirring to dissolve the sugar.

2 Remove from the heat and leave to cool.

3 Purée the mixture with all the remaining ingredients except the oil until smooth. Blend in the oil. Reheat.

Preparation time 5 minutes
Cooking time 10 minutes

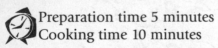

Spicy Orange and Tomato Sauce

Give a lift to carrots or other sweet vegetables with this sauce.

Makes about 450 ml / ¾ pt / 2 cups

	METRIC	IMPERIAL	AMERICAN
Butter	100 g	4 oz	½ cup
Tomato purée (paste)	250 ml	8 fl oz	1 cup
White wine vinegar	250 ml	8 fl oz	1 cup
Horseradish sauce	45 ml	3 tbsp	3 tbsp
Light brown sugar	45 ml	3 tbsp	3 tbsp
Orange juice	60 ml	4 tbsp	4 tbsp
Lemon juice	30 ml	2 tbsp	2 tbsp
Vegetarian Worcestershire Sauce	15 ml	1 tbsp	1 tbsp
Salt			

1 Simmer all the ingredients for about 30 minutes, stirring occasionally, until thick.

2 Serve warm or cold.

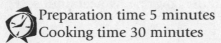
Preparation time 5 minutes
Cooking time 30 minutes

Fresh Tomato Sauce

A basic but tasty sauce to serve hot with pasta, use in other recipes, blend into mayonnaise to make a dip, or serve as a side dressing for simple grilled (broiled) vegetables.

Makes about 300 ml / ½ pt / 1¼ cups

	METRIC	IMPERIAL	AMERICAN
Oil	45 ml	3 tbsp	3 tbsp
Onion, finely chopped	1	1	1
Celery stick, chopped	1	1	1
Carrot, finely chopped	1	1	1
Garlic cloves, crushed	2	2	2
Ripe or canned tomatoes, chopped	450 g	1 lb	1 lb
Water	45 ml	3 tbsp	3 tbsp
Pinch of sugar			
Chopped fresh basil or parsley	15 ml	1 tbsp	1 tbsp
Bay leaf	1	1	1
Salt and freshly ground black pepper			

1   Heat the oil and fry (sauté) the onion, celery, carrot and garlic for a few minutes over a low heat until soft but not browned.

2   Add the remaining ingredients and bring to the boil. Cover and simmer gently for about 20 minutes, stirring occasionally, until the tomatoes are reduced to a pulp.

3   Discard the bay leaf. Purée the sauce, or rub through a sieve (strainer) if you want a smooth texture.

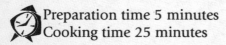
Preparation time 5 minutes
Cooking time 25 minutes

Deep South Sauce

Robust vegetables such as potatoes or fennel are the best accompaniments to this sauce.

Makes about 450 ml / ³/₄ pt / 2 cups

	METRIC	IMPERIAL	AMERICAN
Tomato purée (paste)	250 ml	8 fl oz	1 cup
Garlic clove, crushed	1	1	1
White wine vinegar	150 ml	¼ pt	²/₃ cup
Light brown sugar	75 g	3 oz	¹/₃ cup
Oil	75 ml	5 tbsp	5 tbsp
Vegetarian Worcestershire sauce	30 ml	2 tbsp	2 tbsp
Mustard powder	15 ml	1 tbsp	1 tbsp
Lemon juice	15 ml	1 tbsp	1 tbsp
Salt and freshly ground black pepper			

1 Place all the ingredients in a pan and bring to the boil.

2 Simmer gently for 15 minutes, stirring occasionally.

3 Leave to stand for 2 hours, if possible, before serving hot or cold.

Preparation time 5 minutes
Cooking time 20 minutes
Standing time 2 hours

Quick Chinese Sauce

This sauce will keep in the fridge for several weeks in an airtight jar. It tastes great with rice dishes.

Makes about 450 ml / ¾ pt / 2 cups

	METRIC	IMPERIAL	AMERICAN
Hoisin sauce	250 ml	8 fl oz	1 cup
Rice wine or white wine vinegar	120 ml	4 fl oz	½ cup
Garlic cloves, crushed	2–3	2–3	2–3
Soy sauce	60 ml	4 tbsp	4 tbsp
Chopped fresh root ginger	15 ml	1 tbsp	1 tbsp
Chinese five-spice powder	5 ml	1 tsp	1 tsp

1 Simmer all the ingredients over a low heat for 10 minutes.

2 Serve hot or warm.

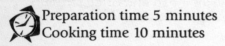
Preparation time 5 minutes
Cooking time 10 minutes

Mustard Sauce

Potatoes or sweetcorn (corn) taste good with Mustard Sauce.

Makes about 450 ml/ ³/₄ pt/2 cups

	METRIC	IMPERIAL	AMERICAN
White wine vinegar	250 ml	8 fl oz	1 cup
Made mustard	175 ml	6 fl oz	³/₄ cup
Onion, finely chopped	¹/₂	¹/₂	¹/₂
Garlic cloves, crushed	4	4	4
Water	75 ml	5 tbsp	5 tbsp
Tomato purée (paste)	60 ml	4 tbsp	4 tbsp
Paprika	15 ml	1 tbsp	1 tbsp
Cayenne	2.5 ml	¹/₂ tsp	¹/₂ tsp
Salt and freshly ground black pepper			

Gently simmer all the ingredients for about 20 minutes, stirring occasionally, until the onion is soft and the sauce thick.

Preparation time 5 minutes
Cooking time 20 minutes

Tarragon Herb Sauce

Ideal for vegetable burgers or patties.

Makes about 350 ml/12 fl oz/1½ cups

	METRIC	IMPERIAL	AMERICAN
Butter or margarine	15 g	½ oz	1 tbsp
Plain (all-purpose) flour	15 g	½ oz	2 tbsp
Milk	300 ml	½ pt	1¼ cups
Chopped fresh tarragon	30 ml	2 tbsp	2 tbsp
Chopped fresh parsley	15 ml	1 tbsp	1 tbsp
Salt and freshly ground black pepper			

1 Melt the butter or margarine, then stir in the flour and cook over a very low heat for 1 minute, stirring.

2 Remove from the heat and stir in the milk until well blended.

3 Return to a low heat and bring to the boil, stirring, then simmer gently for 2 minutes. Stir in the tarragon and parsley and season well with salt and pepper.

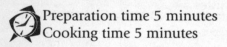 Preparation time 5 minutes
Cooking time 5 minutes

Treacly Apple Sauce

The perfect sauce for barbecued sweetcorn (corn).

Makes about 450 ml/ ³/₄ pt/2 cups

	METRIC	IMPERIAL	AMERICAN
Butter or margarine	50 g	2 oz	¼ cup
Onion, finely chopped	1	1	1
Eating (dessert) apple, peeled and finely chopped	1	1	1
Apple juice	450 ml	³/₄ pt	2 cups
Black treacle (molasses)	30 ml	2 tbsp	2 tbsp
Vegetarian Worcestershire sauce	15 ml	1 tbsp	1 tbsp
Cider vinegar	15 ml	1 tbsp	1 tbsp
Ground cinnamon	5 ml	1 tsp	1 tsp

1 Melt the butter or margarine and fry (sauté) the onion until soft.

2 Stir in the remaining ingredients and mix until well blended.

3 Bring to a boil, then simmer for about 25 minutes until thickened, stirring regularly.

Preparation time 5 minutes
Cooking time 30 minutes

Flavoured Butters

Blend any of these flavour combinations into 100 g/
4 oz/½ cup softened unsalted (sweet) butter, then roll and
chill before slicing on to barbecued vegetables.

* 1 crushed garlic clove, 15 ml/1 tbsp chopped fresh
  herbs (such as parsley, rosemary, tarragon, basil or
  oregano), salt and freshly ground black pepper.

* 15 ml/1 tbsp toasted sesame seeds (see page 19),
  5 ml/1 tsp sesame oil, 1 finely chopped spring onion
  (scallion), salt and freshly ground black pepper.

* 15 ml/1 tbsp chopped fresh mint, 15 ml/1 tbsp made
  mustard, salt and freshly ground black pepper.

* 10 ml/2 tsp chilli powder, a few drops of Tabasco
  sauce, salt and freshly ground black pepper.

* 75 g/3 oz/¾ cup crushed almonds, plenty of salt and a
  little freshly ground black pepper.

* 3 drained, chopped sun-dried tomatoes in oil, 15 ml/
  1 tbsp chopped fresh basil and freshly ground black
  pepper.

* 50 g/2 oz/⅓ cup finely chopped, stoned (pitted) olives,
  10 ml/2 tsp finely chopped capers, 15 ml/1 tbsp
  chopped fresh parsley and freshly ground black pepper.

* 100 g/4 oz/1 cup crumbled blue cheese, a pinch of
  paprika and 30 ml/2 tbsp plain yoghurt.

APPETISERS

Sitting in the fresh air with the smells of the barbecue wafting across the patio is hungry business. If you make sure your guests have plenty to nibble while they are waiting for their main course, they will be less impatient and you will be less flustered. Here is a selection of dishes you can prepare in advance to make life easy, or to cook quickly at the last minute.

Marinated Mozzarella and Olives

A very moreish and easy appetiser.

Serves 4

	METRIC	IMPERIAL	AMERICAN
Mozzarella cheese, cut into chunks	450 g	1 lb	4 cups
Stoned (pitted) black olives	75 g	3 oz	½ cup
Dry white wine	120 ml	4 fl oz	½ cup
Olive oil	120 ml	4 fl oz	½ cup
Lemon juice	30 ml	2 tbsp	2 tbsp
Sun-dried tomatoes in oil, drained and chopped	50 g	2 oz	⅓ cup
Garlic cloves, crushed	2–3	2–3	2–3
Chopped fresh parsley	30 ml	2 tbsp	2 tbsp
Chopped fresh basil	30 ml	2 tbsp	2 tbsp
Pinch of cayenne			
Salt and freshly ground black pepper			
To serve:			
Crusty bread			
Tomato salad			

1   Place the cheese and olives in a large wide-mouthed jar or bowl with a lid.

2   Blend together the remaining ingredients and pour over the cheese and olives.

3   Marinate in the fridge for at least 3 hours, preferably longer.

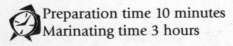
Preparation time 10 minutes
Marinating time 3 hours

Sweet and Sour Tofu

Serves 4

	METRIC	IMPERIAL	AMERICAN
Firm tofu	275 g	10 oz	1 block
Oil	60 ml	4 tbsp	4 tbsp
Soy sauce	150 ml	¼ pt	⅔ cup
Red wine vinegar	30 ml	2 tbsp	2 tbsp
Light brown sugar	60 ml	4 tbsp	4 tbsp
Mustard powder	1.5ml	¼ tsp	¼ tsp
Grated fresh root ginger	15 ml	1 tbsp	1 tbsp
Garlic cloves, crushed	2	2	2

1 Drain the tofu and cut into bite-sized cubes.

2 Mix together the remaining ingredients and pour over the tofu. Cover and chill for 24 hours, turning occasionally.

3 Serve with cocktail sticks (toothpicks).

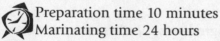
Preparation time 10 minutes
Marinating time 24 hours

Cantonese Mushroom Kebabs

Serves 4

	METRIC	IMPERIAL	AMERICAN
Button mushrooms	225 g	8 oz	½ lb
Can of water chestnuts, drained	230 g	8 oz	1 small
Soy sauce	90 ml	6 tbsp	6 tbsp
Dry sherry	30 ml	2 tbsp	2 tbsp
Groundnut (peanut) oil	30 ml	2 tbsp	2 tbsp
Light brown sugar	15 ml	1 tbsp	1 tbsp
Garlic clove, crushed	1	1	1
Grated fresh root ginger	5 ml	1 tsp	1 tsp
To serve:			
Bean sprouts	175 g	6 oz	6 oz

1 Thread the mushrooms and water chestnuts alternately on soaked wooden skewers. Lay them in a shallow dish.

2 Mix the remaining ingredients together and pour over. Turn to coat completely.

3 Marinate in the fridge for at least 3 hours, preferably overnight.

4 Barbecue for 3–4 minutes until the mushrooms are just tender. Serve the kebabs as a starter on a small pile of bean sprouts.

 Preparation time 10 minutes
Marinating time 3 hours or overnight
Cooking time 3–4 minutes

Chilled Cucumber Soup with Dill

Serves 4

	METRIC	IMPERIAL	AMERICAN
Cucumber	1	1	1
Salt and freshly ground black pepper			
Chopped fresh dill (dill weed)	30 ml	2 tbsp	2 tbsp
Cider vinegar	30 ml	2 tbsp	2 tbsp
Plain yoghurt	300 ml	½ pt	1¼ cups
Milk, cold	300 ml	½ pt	1¼ cups

1 Cut four slices off the cucumber and reserve for garnish. Grate the remainder into a bowl.

2 Sprinkle with salt and leave to stand for 10 minutes. Squeeze out all the moisture and pour away.

3 Add a good grinding of pepper, the dill, vinegar and yoghurt. Chill until ready to serve.

4 Just before serving, stir in the cold milk, ladle into bowls and float a slice of cucumber on each to garnish.

Preparation time 15 minutes plus chilling

Gazpacho

Serves 4

	METRIC	IMPERIAL	AMERICAN
Ripe or canned tomatoes	450 g	1 lb	1 lb
Cucumber, peeled and roughly chopped	1/2	1/2	1/2
Red or green (bell) pepper, quartered 1	1	1	
Onion	1	1	1
Sherry vinegar	15 ml	1 tbsp	1 tbsp
Olive oil	120 ml	4 fl oz	1/2 cup
Fresh breadcrumbs	100 g	4 oz	2 cups
Salt and freshly ground black pepper			
Water			
To serve:			
Ice cubes			

1 Purée all the ingredients except the water together until smooth. Season generously with salt and pepper.

2 Chill well, then thin with water to the consistency you prefer.

3 Serve in a large tureen or individual bowls with ice cubes floating in the soup.

 Preparation time 15 minutes plus chilling

Chilled Spanish Almond Soup

Serves 4

	METRIC	IMPERIAL	AMERICAN
Ground almonds	100 g	4 oz	1 cup
Garlic cloves, crushed	2	2	2
Water	900 ml	1½ pts	3¾ cups
Fresh breadcrumbs	75 g	3 oz	1½ cups
Olive oil	75 ml	5 tbsp	5 tbsp
Sherry vinegar	15 ml	1 tbsp	1 tbsp
Salt and freshly ground black pepper			
To serve:			
Ice cubes			

1 Purée the almonds and garlic with a little of the water to make a paste.

2 Mix in the breadcrumbs, then gradually beat in the oil.

3 Add the vinegar and enough of the remaining water to make the consistency you prefer. Season with salt and pepper.

4 Chill well.

5 Serve in a large tureen or individual bowls with ice cubes floating in the soup.

Preparation time 10 minutes

Special Soup Idea

Of course, you can always serve a hot soup. Choose
something unusual and international from the chill
cabinet of your local supermarket – the choice is
astonishing. Add an interesting garnish of crisp croûtons,
chopped herbs or a swirl of cream and no one will know
you've cheated!

Fabulous Finger Foods

You can always serve crisps, crackers, nuts and other nibbles but here is a range of really tempting titbits.

✳ Slice the tops off cherry tomatoes and scoop out the insides. Fill with garlic and herb soft cheese softened slightly with a little plain yoghurt or milk.

✳ Beat some snipped fresh chives, salt and pepper into cream cheese with a pinch of paprika and pipe or spread on chunks of celery.

✳ Push a stuffed olive into stoned (pitted) ready-to-eat dried apricots or prunes.

✳ Cut very thin slices lengthways from a courgette (zucchini), then roll them round a spoonful of cream cheese flavoured with fresh herbs, a squeeze of lemon juice and some pine nuts.

✳ Alternate chunks of melon and pieces of fresh or semi-dried fig on cocktail sticks (toothpicks) for an interesting combination of flavours and textures.

✳ Spread unsalted (sweet) butter on slices of ciabatta, top with stoned (pitted) sliced black olives and season with lots of black pepper and chopped fresh basil.

✳ Top thick slices of cucumber with a spoonful of garlic-flavoured mayonnaise (see page 138) and a sprig of dill (dill weed).

✳ Make tiny kebabs on cocktail sticks (toothpicks) of cubes of Mozzarella cheese, halved cherry tomatoes and basil leaves.

✳ Spread thin slices of crustless bread with cream cheese. Top with a row of drained mandarin oranges along one edge. Roll up and cut into pinwheels. Try asparagus spears or cooked green beans instead of mandarins.

Guacamole

Serves 4-6

	METRIC	IMPERIAL	AMERICAN
Avocados, peeled, stoned (pitted) and mashed	2	2	2
Garlic clove, crushed	1	1	1
Lemon juice	30 ml	2 tbsp	2 tbsp
Olive oil	15 ml	1 tbsp	1 tbsp
Ground coriander (cilantro)	2.5 ml	½ tsp	½ tsp
A few drops of Tabasco and vegetarian Worcestershire sauce			
Salt and freshly ground black pepper			

1 Purée all the ingredients in a food processor.

2 Taste and adjust the seasoning as you prefer.

 Preparation time 5 minutes

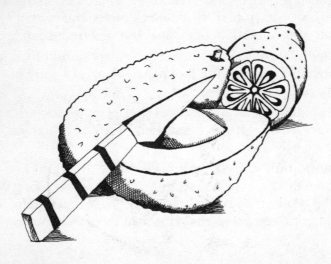

Brandied Blue Cheese Dip

Serves 4

	METRIC	IMPERIAL	AMERICAN
Blue cheese, grated or crumbled	100 g	4 oz	1 cup
Butter or margarine	50 g	2 oz	¼ cup
Cream cheese	100 g	4 oz	½ cup
Crème fraîche	90 ml	6 tbsp	6 tbsp
Shallot, finely chopped	1	1	1
Chopped fresh parsley	30 ml	2 tbsp	2 tbsp
Brandy	45 ml	3 tbsp	3 tbsp
A few drops of vegetarian Worcestershire sauce			
Pinch of sugar			
Salt and freshly ground black pepper			

1 Blend all the ingredients together well.

2 Chill before serving.

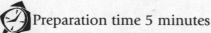 Preparation time 5 minutes

Minted Cream Dip

Serves 4

	METRIC	IMPERIAL	AMERICAN
Soured (dairy sour) cream	250 ml	8 fl oz	1 cup
Chopped fresh mint	30 ml	2 tbsp	2 tbsp
Salt and freshly ground black pepper			

1 Blend all the ingredients together well.

2 Season to taste with mint, salt and pepper.

 Preparation time 5 minutes

Tomato Dip

Serves 4

	METRIC	IMPERIAL	AMERICAN
Can of tomatoes, drained and chopped	200 g	7 oz	1 small
Tomato purée (paste)	45 ml	3 tbsp	3 tbsp
Chopped fresh basil	15 ml	1 tbsp	1 tbsp
A few drops of vegetarian Worcestershire sauce			
Salt and freshly ground black pepper			

1 Blend all the ingredients together well.

2 Season with Worcestershire sauce, salt and pepper.

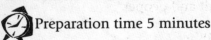 Preparation time 5 minutes

Herb and Lemon Dip

Serves 4

	METRIC	IMPERIAL	AMERICAN
Crème fraîche	250 ml	8 fl oz	1 cup
Chopped fresh parsley	60 ml	4 tbsp	4 tbsp
Chopped fresh dill (dill weed)	60 ml	4 tbsp	4 tbsp
Snipped fresh chives	30 ml	2 tbsp	2 tbsp
Lemon juice	15 ml	1 tbsp	1 tbsp
Salt and freshly ground black pepper			

1 Blend all the ingredients together well.

2 Season to taste with salt and pepper.

Preparation time 5 minutes

Cheesy Gherkin Dip

Serves 4

	METRIC	IMPERIAL	AMERICAN
Plain yoghurt	250 ml	8 fl oz	1 cup
Strong cheese, grated	75 g	3 oz	¾ cup
Gherkins (cornichons), drained and chopped	2	2	2
Salt and freshly ground black pepper			

1 Blend all the ingredients together well.

2 Season to taste with salt and pepper.

Preparation time 5 minutes

Aubergine Caviare

Serves 4

	METRIC	IMPERIAL	AMERICAN
Aubergines (eggplants)	2	2	2
Small onion, finely chopped	1	1	1
Ripe tomatoes, skinned and finely chopped	3	3	3
Garlic clove, crushed	1	1	1
Olive oil	60 ml	4 tbsp	4 tbsp
Salt and freshly ground black pepper			
A little lemon juice (optional)			
To garnish:			
Chopped fresh parsley or coriander (cilantro)			
To serve:			
Warm cocktail-sized pitta breads			

1 Cut off and discard the prickly aubergine stalks. Place under a hot grill (broiler) and grill (broil) for 20 minutes until blackened, turning occasionally.

2 Cut in halves and scoop out all the softened flesh with a spoon and discard the skins.

3 Finely chop the flesh and place in a bowl. Stir in the onion, tomato and garlic. Work in the olive oil, a little at a time, then season to taste and sharpen slightly with lemon juice, if liked. Spoon into a small serving dish. Sprinkle with chopped parsley or coriander and serve with warm cocktail-sized pitta breads to dip in.

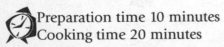
Preparation time 10 minutes
Cooking time 20 minutes

More Dip Ideas

The easiest choice for dips has to be to buy a selection of vegetarian dips from the supermarket – and why not? There's a great range and they taste good. But they are so easy to make, and usually taste better when you have made them yourself as you can add that bit of extra seasoning or interesting variation. All you need is a food processor – or you can chop the ingredients finely for a coarser texture.

* **Mandarin and almond dip:** mix 120 ml/4 fl oz/½ cup mayonnaise (see page 138) with 300 g/11 oz canned drained mandarins, 2.5 ml/½ tsp curry powder, 25 g/1 oz/¼ cup chopped almonds and 5 ml/1 tsp lemon juice.

* **Cream cheese and avocado dip:** purée the flesh of an avocado with 1 garlic clove, 225 g/8 oz/1 cup cream cheese, 15 ml/1 tbsp lemon juice and 15 ml/1 tbsp snipped fresh chives.

* Flavour mayonnaise (see page 138), or fromage frais, or cream cheese, or thick plain yoghurt (or a combination) to taste with one of the following: grain mustard; chopped fresh herbs; crushed garlic; chopped gherkins (cornichons); tomato chutney and a few drops of vegetarian Worcestershire sauce; cayenne or chilli powder; curry powder.

Interesting Dunkers

You need a choice of fresh and crunchy vegetables or biscuits to serve with your dips. Here are some ideas.

* A bowl of raw vegetables cut into thin julienne strips makes a colourful table centre and the perfect accompaniment to a selection of dips. Go for all the old favourites if you like them: carrot, cucumber, celery and (bell) peppers.

* Don't ignore other vegetables that give you a more unusual selection. Try tiny cauliflower and broccoli florets, baby carrots, sugarsnap peas, mangetout (snow peas), chicory (Belgian endive), different mushrooms or pieces of blanched asparagus.

* Fruits also offer an interesting counterpoint. Try pieces of star fruit, pear, apple, melon, pineapple, peach or apricot.

* Tortilla chips, corn chips, grissini and strips of pitta bread are also great for dipping.

* Try fingers of bread, fried (sautéed) until golden and crisp in olive oil with a clove of garlic.

* Cheese straws, either bought or home-made.

* Cut the peelings of well-scrubbed potatoes in short lengths. Spread on a baking sheet and sprinkle with salt. Bake in a preheated oven at 200°C/400°F/gas mark 6 for 20 minutes until crisp. Toss and serve warm or cold.

Crispy Potato Skins

Quantities don't really matter for this dish – just be warned to make twice as much as you think you will need as they are very moreish. I allow at least one potato per person.

	METRIC	IMPERIAL	AMERICAN
Potatoes			
Olive oil			
Coarsely ground salt			
Freshly ground black pepper			

1 Bake the potatoes in a preheated oven at 200°C/ 400°F/gas mark 6 for about 1 hour or until soft to the touch. Alternatively, pierce the skins with a fork and microwave until tender; four potatoes will take about 12 minutes on high. Leave to cool slightly.

2 Cut the potatoes into quarters and scoop out most of the insides, leaving the skins and a layer of potato.

3 Arrange the potato skins in a shallow flameproof pan, brush them generously with olive oil, then sprinkle with lots of salt and a little pepper or cayenne. Return to the hot oven for about 20 minutes, or barbecue until browned and crisp, turning and brushing again once or twice.

4 Use the potato flesh for: mashed potatoes; mixed with chopped onion, shaped into little cakes and fried (sautéed); mixed with cooked greens to make Bubble and Squeak; sliced or crumbled into an ovenproof dish with a cheese or white sauce, sprinkled with a mixture of grated strong cheese and breadcrumbs and baked until crisp and golden.

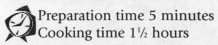
Preparation time 5 minutes
Cooking time 1½ hours

Fake Foccaccia

Serves 4

	METRIC	IMPERIAL	AMERICAN
Olive oil	45 ml	3 tbsp	3 tbsp
Onions, sliced	6	6	6
Garlic cloves, chopped	3	3	3
Pitta breads	4	4	4
Salt and freshly ground black pepper			

1 Heat the oil and fry (sauté) the onions and garlic until soft but not browned.

2 Brush the pitta breads on one side with a little more oil. Pile the onion and garlic mixture on top and season generously with salt and pepper.

3 Grill (broil) under a hot grill (broiler) for about 5 minutes until browned on top.

Preparation time 5 minutes
Cooking time 15 minutes

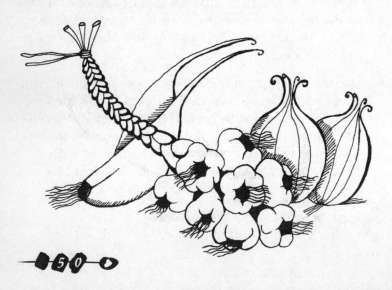

Grilled Avocado

Serves 4

	METRIC	IMPERIAL	AMERICAN
Avocados	2	2	2
Grated rind and juice of 1 lime			
Butter or margarine, melted	45 ml	3 tbsp	3 tbsp
Salt and freshly ground black pepper			
Chopped fresh parsley	30 ml	2 tbsp	2 tbsp
Fromage frais	60 ml	4 tbsp	4 tbsp

1 Peel and stone (pit) the avocados and sprinkle with lime juice. Cut into thick slices.

2 Brush generously with butter or margarine, sprinkle with lime rind and season with salt and pepper.

3 Barbecue or grill (broil) for about 2 minutes on each side until lightly browned. Serve sprinkled with parsley with a spoonful of fromage frais.

Preparation time 5 minutes
Cooking time 5 minutes

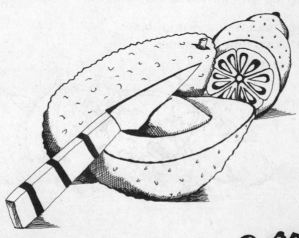

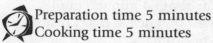

Breaded Button Mushroons

Serves 4

	METRIC	IMPERIAL	AMERICAN
Button mushrooms	450 g	1 lb	1 lb
Plain (all-purpose) flour	30 ml	2 tbsp	2 tbsp
Salt and freshly ground black pepper			
Egg, beaten	1	1	1
Fine breadcrumbs	50 g	2 oz	1 cup
Oil for deep-frying			
Flavoured mayonnaise (see page 138)			

1 Dust the mushrooms in seasoned flour, shaking off any excess.

2 Dip in the beaten egg, then in breadcrumbs until well covered.

3 Fry (sauté) in hot oil for about 4 minutes until golden brown. Drain well on kitchen paper before serving with flavoured mayonnaise.

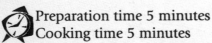

Preparation time 5 minutes
Cooking time 5 minutes

Savoury Cheese Twists

Makes about 60

	METRIC	IMPERIAL	AMERICAN
Frozen puff pastry, thawed	250 g	9 oz	1 packet
Yeast extract	15 ml	1 tbsp	1 tbsp
Cheddar cheese, finely grated	50 g	2 oz	½ cup
To glaze:			
Beaten egg	1	1	1

1 Roll out the pastry on a lightly floured surface to a 30 cm/12 in square.

2 Spread the yeast extract over, then sprinkle with the cheese.

3 Fold the square in half and roll over again lightly with the rolling pin to seal in the filling.

4 Brush lightly with beaten egg, then cut into thin strips.

5 Hold each end of a strip and twist, then place on a dampened baking sheet. Repeat with each strip.

6 Bake in a preheated oven at 220°C/425°F/gas mark 7 for about 10 minutes until crisp and golden. Serve warm or cold.

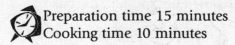
Preparation time 15 minutes
Cooking time 10 minutes

Rustic Olive Bites

Serves 4

	METRIC	IMPERIAL	AMERICAN
French bread slices	3	3	3
Olive oil	45 ml	3 tbsp	3 tbsp
Button mushrooms, finely chopped	175 g	6 oz	6 oz
Small garlic clove, crushed	1	1	1
Salt and freshly ground black pepper			
Squeeze of lemon juice			
Black olives, stoned (pitted)	40 g	1½ oz	¼ cup
Pine nuts	15 ml	1 tbsp	1 tbsp
Chopped fresh basil	10 ml	2 tsp	2 tsp

1   Put the bread on a baking sheet and bake in a preheated oven at 180°C/350°F/gas mark 4 until golden brown.

2   Meanwhile, heat half the oil in a frying pan (skillet) and fry (sauté) the mushrooms and garlic for 4 minutes until tender. Season to taste with salt, pepper and a dash of lemon juice. Cook rapidly, if necessary, for a few seconds to evaporate any juices. Remove from the heat.

3   Purée the olives in a blender or food processor with the remaining oil, the pine nuts and half the basil.

4   When ready to serve, spread the olive mixture on the toasted bread and top with the chopped mushrooms. Sprinkle with the remaining basil and serve.

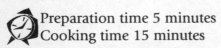
Preparation time 5 minutes
Cooking time 15 minutes

STRAIGHT ON THE BARBECUE

Many vegetables can be placed straight on the barbecue with the most wonderful results – simple barbecued onions have quite a different taste from when they are cooked in any other way. Choose firm vegetables so that they don't fall apart during cooking. Some vegetables are best par-boiled before you start so that you can ensure that melt-in-the-mouth centre and crispy outside.

Vegetarian burgers and sausages, and other similar dishes, are best cooked in a hinged wire grille so that they are held firmly together and don't disintegrate during cooking.

~~~~~~~~~~~

Nutty Celeriac

Serves 4

	METRIC	IMPERIAL	AMERICAN
Celeriac (celery root)	1	1	1
White wine vinegar	15 ml	1 tbsp	1 tbsp
Oil	90 ml	6 tbsp	6 tbsp
Ground walnuts	50 g	2 oz	½ cup

1 Peel the celeriac and cut it into 2.5 cm/1 in slices and boil for about 10 minutes until just tender. Drain well.

2 Mix together the remaining ingredients and brush over the celeriac. Leave to stand for about 30 minutes,

3 Barbecue for about 5 minutes until crispy.

Preparation time 5 minutes
Marinating time 30 minutes
Cooking time 15 minutes

Grilled Chicory

Serves 4

	METRIC	IMPERIAL	AMERICAN
Chicory (Belgian endive) heads	4	4	4
Oil	30 ml	2 tbsp	2 tbsp
Butter or margarine, melted	30 ml	2 tbsp	2 tbsp
Chopped mixed fresh herbs	30 ml	2 tbsp	2 tbsp
Salt and freshly ground black pepper			

1 Cut a cone-shaped core out of the base of each chicory head, then slice in half lengthways.

2 Mix together the oil, butter or margarine, herbs, salt and pepper and brush over the chicory.

3 Barbecue for about 10 minutes, turning and basting with more oil mixture as it cooks.

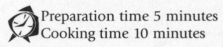

Preparation time 5 minutes
Cooking time 10 minutes

Fennel with Caraway

Serves 4

	METRIC	IMPERIAL	AMERICAN
Fennel bulbs, thickly sliced	4	4	4
Butter or margarine, melted	45 ml	3 tbsp	3 tbsp
Caraway seeds	15 ml	1 tbsp	1 tbsp
Salt and freshly ground black pepper			
Grated Parmesan cheese	50 g	2 oz	½ cup

1 Cook the fennel in boiling water for about 6 minutes until just tender. Drain well, then leave to cool.

2 Brush the fennel with butter, sprinkle with caraway seeds and season with salt and pepper.

3 Barbecue for about 2 minutes on each side until lightly browned. Transfer to a serving dish and sprinkle with Parmesan.

Preparation time 5 minutes
Cooking time 10 minutes

Nutty Burgers

Serves 4

	METRIC	IMPERIAL	AMERICAN
Bulghar wheat	175 g	6 oz	1 cup
Water	1 litre	1¾ pts	4¼ cups
Salt and freshly ground black pepper			
Cornmeal	100 g	4 oz	1 cup
Peanut butter	15 ml	1 tbsp	1 tbsp
Salted peanuts, finely chopped	75 g	3 oz	¾ cup
Oil	45 ml	3 tbsp	3 tbsp

1   Place the bulghar in a heavy pan and heat gently for a few minutes until it is lightly browned, shaking the pan as it heats.

2   Pour in 450 ml/¾ pt/2 cups of the water, stir well and bring to the boil. Cover and simmer for 20 minutes, stirring occasionally to prevent it sticking. Season with salt and pepper.

3   Bring the remaining water to the boil in a large pan, stir in the cornmeal, peanut butter, and a little salt and pepper. Cover and simmer very gently for 30 minutes, stirring frequently, until the mixture is firm and comes away from the sides of the pan. Stir in the peanuts. Leave to cool.

4   Mix together the cornmeal mixture with the bulghar and shape into burgers. Chill well.

5   Brush the burgers with oil and barbecue in a hinged wire grille for about 5 minutes on each side.

Preparation time 10 minutes
Cooking time 40 minutes plus chilling

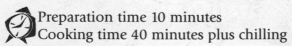

Brilliant Veggie Burgers

Serves 4

	METRIC	IMPERIAL	AMERICAN
Rolled oats	100 g	4 oz	1 cup
Wholemeal flour	75 g	3 oz	¾ cup
Celery sticks, finely chopped	2	2	2
Carrots, grated	2	2	2
Small parsnip, grated	1	1	1
Cheddar cheese, grated	50 g	2 oz	½ cup
Small onion, finely chopped	1	1	1
Tomato purée (paste)	15 ml	1 tbsp	1 tbsp
Soy sauce	15 ml	1 tbsp	1 tbsp
Dried oregano	5 ml	1 tsp	1 tsp
Salt and freshly ground black pepper			
Egg, beaten	1	1	1
Oil			

1 Mix all the ingredients except the oil thoroughly together. Shape into four burgers and chill until ready to cook.

2 Place in a hinged wire grille and brush with oil. Barbecue for about 5 minutes on each side until golden brown and cooked through. Serve hot.

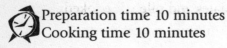 Preparation time 10 minutes
Cooking time 10 minutes

Nice 'n' Nutty Burgers

Prepare as for Brilliant Veggie Burgers (left) but substitute 50 g/2 oz/½ cup of chopped mixed nuts for half the rolled oats.

~~~~~~~~~~~~~~~~

Grilled Garlic Peppers

Serves 4

	METRIC	IMPERIAL	AMERICAN
Red, yellow or green (bell) peppers	3	3	3
Oil	90 ml	6 tbsp	6 tbsp
Garlic cloves, crushed	2	2	2
Dried thyme	5 ml	1 tsp	1 tsp
Pinch of cayenne			
French bread slices	4	4	4

1   Cut the peppers into quarters or large strips.

2   Mix together the remaining ingredients and brush over the peppers.

3   Barbecue for about 10 minutes, turning and brushing frequently with the flavoured oil.

4   When the peppers are half-cooked, brush the bread with some of the oil and barbecue until browned on both sides. Place on plates and pile the cooked pepper strips on top.

Preparation time 5 minutes
Cooking time 20 minutes

Black Eye Bean and Cashew Burgers

Serves 4

	METRIC	IMPERIAL	AMERICAN
Dried black eye beans, soaked overnight in cold water	175 g	6 oz	1½ cups
Carrot, grated	1	1	1
Turnip, grated	1	1	1
Cashew nuts, chopped	25 g	1 oz	¼ cup
Wholemeal breadcrumbs	50 g	2 oz	1 cup
Yeast extract	2.5 ml	½ tsp	½ tsp
Vegetarian Worcestershire sauce	2.5 ml	½ tsp	½ tsp
Egg, beaten	1	1	1
Salt and freshly ground black pepper			
A little oil			

1   Drain the beans and place in a saucepan. Cover with cold water. Bring to the boil and boil rapidly for 10 minutes. Reduce the heat, part-cover and simmer gently for 1 hour. Drain and mash thoroughly.

2   When cool enough to handle, mix in all the remaining ingredients except the oil, seasoning with a little salt and pepper.

3   With floured hands, shape into four burgers. Chill for at least 30 minutes.

4   When ready to cook, place in a hinged wire grille and brush with oil. Barbecue until golden brown on both sides.

 Preparation time 1 hour plus soaking
Cooking time 10 minutes

Leeks or Onions with Basil Butter

Serves 4

	METRIC	IMPERIAL	AMERICAN
Leeks or onions	4	4	4
Tomatoes, halved	4	4	4
Olive oil	30 ml	2 tbsp	2 tbsp
Lemon juice	15 ml	1 tbsp	1 tbsp
Salt and freshly ground black pepper			
For the basil butter:			
Butter or margarine, softened	40 g	1½ oz	3 tbsp
Garlic clove, crushed	1	1	1
Chopped fresh basil	15 ml	1 tbsp	1 tbsp

1 Trim the leeks and cut them in half lengthways, or trim and halve the onions. Brush the leeks or onions and the tomatoes with olive oil.

2 Barbecue the leeks for about 3 minutes on each side, or onions for about 6 minutes on each side, until just soft and lightly browned, and the tomatoes for about 2 minutes on each side.

3 Transfer to a serving dish and sprinkle with the lemon juice, salt and pepper.

4 Meanwhile, blend the butter or margarine with the garlic and basil and season with salt and pepper. Dot over the vegetables and serve.

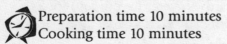

Preparation time 10 minutes
Cooking time 10 minutes

Spiced Herb Onions

Serves 4

	METRIC	IMPERIAL	AMERICAN
Small onions	450 g	1 lb	1 lb
For the basting mixture:			
Chopped fresh parsley	45 ml	3 tbsp	3 tbsp
Finely chopped spring onions (scallions)	4	4	4
Dried mixed herbs	5 ml	1 tsp	1 tsp
Mustard powder	2.5 ml	½ tsp	½ tsp
A few drops of chilli sauce			
Salt and freshly ground black pepper			
Butter or margarine, softened	225 g	8 oz	1 cup

1 Mix together the seasoning ingredients for the basting mixture and blend them into the butter or margarine. Chill until ready to cook.

2 Brush the onions generously with the mixture, then continue to brush as you barbecue them for about 20 minutes until tender.

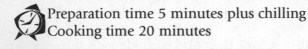 Preparation time 5 minutes plus chilling
Cooking time 20 minutes

Barbecued Red Onions

Try barbecuing red onions, quartered and brushed with olive oil. They have a slightly sweeter flavour and look spectacular. Use them thinly sliced in salads, too.

Greek-style Barbecued Peppers

Serves 4

	METRIC	IMPERIAL	AMERICAN
Red (bell) pepper	1	1	1
Green pepper	1	1	1
Orange pepper	1	1	1
Yellow pepper	1	1	1
Olive oil	45 ml	3 tbsp	3 tbsp
Chopped fresh basil	15 ml	1 tbsp	1 tbsp
Salt and freshly ground black pepper			
Feta cheese, cubed	100 g	4 oz	1 cup
Greek black olives	8	8	8

1 Remove the stalk and seeds from the peppers, but leave them intact. Brush with some of the olive oil.

2 Barbecue for about 10 minutes, turning frequently until the peppers are soft and the skin is charred.

3 Wrap in a paper or thick plastic bag and seal the top to keep the steam inside. Leave for about 10 minutes until the peppers are just cool enough to handle.

4 Peel off the skin and tear the peppers into strips.

5 Place in a bowl and sprinkle with the remaining oil, the basil, salt and pepper and the cheese. Garnish with olives and serve straight away.

Preparation time 15 minutes
Cooking time 10 minutes

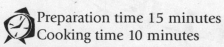

Potato Wedges

Serves 4

	METRIC	IMPERIAL	AMERICAN
Large potatoes, scrubbed	4	4	4
Salt			
Butter or margarine, softened	75 g	3 oz	⅓ cup
Garlic cloves, crushed	2	2	2
Chopped fresh basil	15 ml	1 tbsp	1 tbsp
Freshly ground black pepper			

1 Cook the potatoes in boiling salted water until just tender. Drain and cut into large wedges.

2 Mix the butter or margarine with the garlic, basil, pepper and a little salt, if liked. Brush over the potatoes.

3 Barbecue the potatoes, on a piece of foil if this is easier, for about 6–10 minutes until golden.

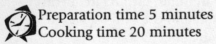
Preparation time 5 minutes
Cooking time 20 minutes

Sweet Potatoes with Nutty Butter

These take some time to cook but need no attention.

Serves 4

	METRIC	IMPERIAL	AMERICAN
Sweet potatoes	4	4	4
Butter or margarine	100 g	4 oz	½ cup
Clear honey	5 ml	1 tsp	1 tsp
Grated rind and juice of 1 orange			
Walnuts, chopped	25 g	1 oz	¼ cup
Pinch of mustard powder			
Salt and freshly ground black pepper			

1   Pierce the skin of the potatoes and cook them in the oven at 200°C/400°F/gas mark 6 for about 1 hour until soft, in the microwave on high for about 12 minutes (or according to manufacturers' instructions), or on the barbecue for about 2 hours.

2   Melt all the remaining ingredients together in a pan and keep hot.

3   To serve, split open the potatoes and spoon over the flavoured butter.

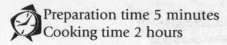
Preparation time 5 minutes
Cooking time 2 hours

Spinach-stuffed Mushrooms

Serves 4

	METRIC	IMPERIAL	AMERICAN
Large flat mushrooms	8	8	8
Butter or margarine	25 g	1 oz	2 tbsp
Oil	15 ml	1 tbsp	1 tbsp
Onion, chopped	1	1	1
Garlic cloves, chopped	2	2	2
Frozen spinach, thawed and drained	225 g	8 oz	½ lb
Vegetable stock	90 ml	6 tbsp	6 tbsp
Salt and freshly ground black pepper			
Curd (smooth cottage) cheese	100 g	4 oz	½ cup
Dry breadcrumbs	45 ml	3 tbsp	3 tbsp
Parmesan cheese, freshly grated	50 g	2 oz	½ cup

1 Remove the mushroom stalks and chop them finely.

2 Heat the butter or margarine and oil and fry (sauté) the onion and garlic until soft. Stir in the mushroom stalks, spinach and stock and season well. Remove from the heat and stir in the curd cheese.

3 Place the mushroom caps, gill-side up, and pile the mixture on top. Sprinkle with breadcrumbs and Parmesan. Barbecue for about 10 minutes until cooked through and bubbling.

Preparation time 5 minutes
Cooking time 25 minutes

Sweetcorn with Lime and Chilli Butter

Serves 4

	METRIC	IMPERIAL	AMERICAN
Sweetcorn (corn) on cobs	4	4	4
Butter, softened	175 g	6 oz	¾ cup
Lime juice	45 ml	3 tbsp	3 tbsp
Chilli powder	10 ml	2 tsp	2 tsp
Salt			

1 Leave the sweetcorn in the husks. Soak in cold water for at least 20 minutes.

2 Beat together the butter, lime juice and chilli powder to taste and season to taste with salt. Roll the flavoured butter into a sausage shape in greaseproof (waxed) paper and chill.

3 Drain the corn and barbecue in the husks for about 20 minutes until the husks are evenly browned.

4 Remove from the barbecue and carefully take off the husks and silks. Serve with the flavoured butter cut into slices.

Preparation time 5 minutes plus soaking
Cooking time 20 minutes

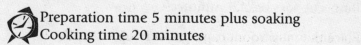

Sage and Onion Tomatoes

Substitute parsley and thyme or any other of your favourite herbs for the sage.

Serves 4

	METRIC	IMPERIAL	AMERICAN
Beefsteak tomatoes, halved	4	4	4
Salt and freshly ground black pepper			
Onion, finely chopped	1	1	1
Butter or margarine	15 g	½ oz	1 tbsp
Fresh breadcrumbs	50 g	2 oz	1 cup
Chopped fresh sage	5 ml	1 tsp	1 tsp
Strong cheese, grated	100 g	4 oz	1 cup

1 Scoop out the seeds from the tomato halves and season with salt and pepper.

2 Fry (sauté) the onion in the butter or margarine for 3 minutes to soften. Stir in the breadcrumbs and sage and season with salt and pepper.

3 Pile the stuffing mixture back into the tomato halves.

4 Barbecue for about 5 minutes.

5 Top the tomatoes with the grated cheese and barbecue for a further 5 minutes until melted.

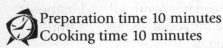
Preparation time 10 minutes
Cooking time 10 minutes

Spinach and Cheese Patties

Serves 4

	METRIC	IMPERIAL	AMERICAN
Cooked or thawed, frozen spinach	450 g	1 lb	1 lb
Strong cheese, grated	225 g	8 oz	2 cups
Salt and freshly ground black pepper			
Pinch of grated nutmeg			
Egg yolks, beaten	2	2	2
Butter or margarine, melted	15 g	½ oz	1 tbsp
Egg, beaten	1	1	1
Dried breadcrumbs	100 g	4 oz	1 cup
Oil			

1 Place the spinach in a colander and press it down to drain it thoroughly. Chop it finely.

2 Beat in the cheese, a little salt and pepper and the nutmeg.

3 Beat the egg yolks with the butter or margarine and stir into the mixture. Shape into patties.

4 Brush the patties with beaten egg and roll in breadcrumbs, pressing them on firmly until covered. Chill well.

5 Brush both sides of the patties with oil and barbecue in a hinged wire grille for about 10 minutes until crisp and cooked through.

Preparation time 10 minutes plus chilling
Cooking time 10 minutes

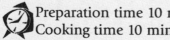

Grilled Vegetables with Peanut Mayonnaise

Serves 4

	METRIC	IMPERIAL	AMERICAN
Aubergine (eggplant)	1	1	1
Courgettes (zucchini)	2	2	2
Red (bell) peppers	2	2	2
Spring onions (scallions)	8	8	8
For the mayonnaise:			
Garlic cloves, crushed	3	3	3
Egg	1	1	1
Peanut butter	15 ml	1 tbsp	1 tbsp
Lime juice	30 ml	2 tbsp	2 tbsp
Olive oil	250 ml	8 fl oz	1 cup
Salt and freshly ground black pepper			

1 Cut the aubergine lengthways into 2.5 cm/1 in thick slices. Sprinkle with salt and leave to stand for 1 hour. Rinse and pat dry.

2 Cut the courgettes lengthways into thick slices, quarter the peppers and trim the spring onions.

3 Make the mayonnaise. Blend together two of the garlic cloves, the egg, peanut butter and lime juice in a blender or food processor. Slowly add half the oil in a steady stream until the mixture thickens. Season to taste with salt and pepper. Leave to stand before serving, if possible.

4   Mix the remaining garlic and oil and brush over the vegetables.

5   Barbecue for about 10 minutes, turning and brushing regularly, until cooked through and browned. Serve with the peanut mayonnaise.

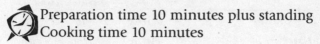 Preparation time 10 minutes plus standing
Cooking time 10 minutes

Barbecued Chips

Serves 4

	METRIC	IMPERIAL	AMERICAN
Good handfuls of frozen chips	4	4	4
Groundnut (peanut) oil	30 ml	2 tbsp	2 tbsp
Coarse sea salt	5 ml	1 tsp	1 tsp

1   Lay a double thickness of foil on part of the barbecue and spread the chips in a single layer.

2   Drizzle with the oil and barbecue, turning occasionally until browned and crisp.

3   Sprinkle with coarse sea salt and serve.

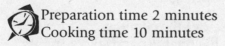 Preparation time 2 minutes
Cooking time 10 minutes

Spicy Chips

Prepare as for Barbecued Chips (above) but sprinkle with 5 ml/1 tsp of ground cumin and 1.5 ml/¼ tsp of chilli powder, mixed with the salt.

Potato and Coriander Burgers

Serves 4

	METRIC	IMPERIAL	AMERICAN
Potatoes	750 g	1½ lb	1½ lb
Split red lentils	50 g	2 oz	⅓ cup
Oil	30 ml	2 tbsp	2 tbsp
Cumin seeds, crushed	2.5 ml	½ tsp	½ tsp
Finely chopped onion	30 ml	2 tbsp	2 tbsp
Chopped fresh coriander (cilantro)	45 ml	3 tbsp	3 tbsp
Ground coriander	1.5 ml	¼ tsp	¼ tsp
Pinch of ground cumin			
Pinch of cayenne			
Salt and freshly ground black pepper			
Flour for dusting			
Oil for brushing			

1   Boil the potatoes in their skins, leave to cool slightly, then peel and mash.

2   Boil the lentils in water to cover, for about 30 minutes until soft, then drain thoroughly.

3   Heat the oil and fry (sauté) the cumin seeds for a few seconds. Add the onion, coriander and spices and fry for 2 minutes.

4   Stir in the lentils, season with salt and pepper and simmer, stirring frequently, until the mixture is dry. Leave to cool.

5 Divide each mixture into eight pieces and shape into rounds. Press a ball of lentil filling into each ball of potato and shape gently into patties. Dust with flour and chill until firm.

6 Brush the patties with oil and barbecue in a hinged wire grille for about 10 minutes until golden brown.

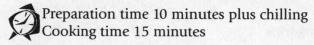

Preparation time 10 minutes plus chilling
Cooking time 15 minutes

Outdoor Tomatoes

Serves 4

	METRIC	IMPERIAL	AMERICAN
Beefsteak tomatoes, halved	2	2	2
Butter or margarine	25 g	1 oz	2 tbsp
Spring onions (scallions), finely chopped	2	2	2
Chopped fresh parsley	15 ml	1 tbsp	1 tbsp
Dried basil	5 ml	1 tsp	1 tsp
Salt and freshly ground black pepper			

1 Place the four tomato halves on a square of foil, shiny side up. Mash together the remaining ingredients and smear over the tomatoes.

2 Barbecue for about 15 minutes or until the tomatoes are soft but still hold their shape. Serve straight away.

Preparation time 10 minutes
Cooking time 15 minutes

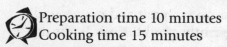

Cheesy Grilled Polenta

Serves 4

	METRIC	IMPERIAL	AMERICAN
Water	900 ml	1½ pts	3¾ cups
Salt	10 ml	2 tsp	2 tsp
Polenta	225 g	8 oz	2 cups
Butter or margarine	75 g	3 oz	⅓ cup
Parmesan or other strong cheese, grated	50 g	2 oz	½ cup
Olive oil	60 ml	4 tbsp	4 tbsp
To serve:			
Grated cheese			
Sprigs of basil			

1 Bring the water and salt to the boil, gradually add the polenta and stir until the mixture begins to thicken. Simmer very gently, stirring occasionally, for about 20 minutes until thick.

2 Stir in the butter or margarine and the cheese. Spoon into a Swiss roll tin (jelly roll pan) or a square shallow tin so that the polenta is about 2.5 cm/1 in thick. Leave to cool, then chill.

3 When ready to cook, cut the polenta into squares and brush with oil.

4 Barbecue for about 5 minutes on each side until golden brown. Serve sprinkled with more cheese and sprigs of fresh basil.

Preparation time 5 minutes plus chilling
Cooking time 25 minutes

Spiced Baby Carrots and Corn

Serves 4

	METRIC	IMPERIAL	AMERICAN
Whole baby carrots, trimmed, leaving a short stalk	100 g	4 oz	¼ lb
Baby corn cobs	100 g	4 oz	¼ lb
Butter or margarine, melted	50 g	2 oz	¼ cup
Salt and freshly ground black pepper			
Ground cumin	1.5 ml	¼ tsp	¼ tsp

1 Toss the vegetables in the melted fat, seasoned with a little salt and pepper and the cumin.

2 Spread out on a sheet of foil on the barbecue and cook for about 5 minutes, turning frequently and brushing with the melted fat, until just tender and lightly browned.

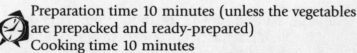

Preparation time 10 minutes (unless the vegetables are prepacked and ready-prepared)
Cooking time 10 minutes

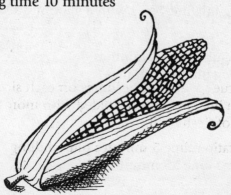

Barbecued Butternut Squash

Serves 4

	METRIC	IMPERIAL	AMERICAN
Butternut squash	2	2	2
Butter or margarine	50 g	2 oz	¼ cup
Grated rind and juice of 1 orange			
Light soy sauce	10 ml	2 tsp	2 tsp
Freshly ground black pepper			

1 Cut the squash in halves lengthways. Scoop out the seeds (pits).

2 Melt the butter or margarine and stir in the orange rind and juice, the soy sauce and some freshly ground black pepper.

3 Brush the squash halves with some of the melted mixture.

4 Barbecue, skin side down, for about 45 minutes or until the flesh is tender, brushing frequently with the basting mixture. Serve with a spoon to scoop out the flesh.

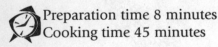
Preparation time 8 minutes
Cooking time 45 minutes

KEBABS

Vegetables, Quorn and tofu make wonderful kebabs. The golden rules with vegetables are to choose those that will take about the same length of time to cook, and to cut them into similar-sized pieces so that they cook evenly. Baste the kebabs well with oil, butter or a marinade and turn them frequently while they are cooking. The only limit is your own imagination.

〜〜〜〜〜〜〜〜

Vegetable Fajitas

Serves 4

	METRIC	IMPERIAL	AMERICAN
Ripe or canned tomatoes, diced	450 g	1 lb	1 lb
Onion, finely chopped	1	1	1
Fresh green chillies, finely chopped	4	4	4
Chopped fresh coriander (cilantro)	60 ml	4 tbsp	4 tbsp
Garlic clove, crushed	1	1	1
Lime juice	30 ml	2 tbsp	2 tbsp
Salt and freshly ground black pepper			
Aubergine (eggplant)	1	1	1
Green (bell) pepper	1	1	1
Red onion	1	1	1
Cherry tomatoes	225 g	8 oz	½ lb
Button mushrooms	225 g	8 oz	½ lb
Oil	90 ml	6 tbsp	6 tbsp
Tortillas	12	12	12

1   Make the salsa up to two days in advance. Mix together the first six ingredients and season to taste with salt and pepper.

2   Cut the aubergine, pepper and onion into 2 cm/¾ in cubes. Thread alternately on to soaked wooden skewers with the tomatoes and mushrooms.

3   Season the oil with salt and pepper and brush over the vegetables.

4   Barbecue for about 8 minutes, turning frequently and continuing to brush with seasoned oil as they cook.

5   Meanwhile, warm the tortillas at the side of the barbecue.

6   To serve, slide the vegetables off the skewers on to the hot tortillas and top with the tomato salsa.

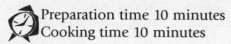 Preparation time 10 minutes
Cooking time 10 minutes

Courgette Ribbons Vinaigrette

Serves 4

	METRIC	IMPERIAL	AMERICAN
Courgettes (zucchini)	450 g	1 lb	1 lb
Olive oil	30 ml	2 tbsp	2 tbsp
White wine vinegar	5 ml	1 tsp	1 tsp
Garlic clove, crushed	1	1	1
Chopped fresh parsley	15 ml	1 tbsp	1 tbsp
Salt and freshly ground black pepper			

1   Use a potato peeler to cut the courgettes into long thin ribbons. Place two or three ribbons on top of each other, then thread them on to soaked wooden skewers, folding them backwards and forwards like a concertina.

2   Whisk together the oil, vinegar, garlic and parsley, salt and pepper. Brush over the courgettes.

3   Barbecue for about 8–10 minutes, turning and basting.

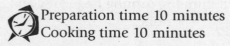 Preparation time 10 minutes
Cooking time 10 minutes

Curried Coconut Cauliflower

Serves 4

	METRIC	IMPERIAL	AMERICAN
Garlic clove, crushed	1	1	1
Canned coconut milk	300 ml	½ pt	1¼ cups
Desiccated (shredded) coconut	50 g	2 oz	½ cup
Curry powder	15 ml	1 tbsp	1 tbsp
Lemon juice	10 ml	2 tsp	2 tsp
Pinch of cayenne			
Salt and freshly ground black pepper			
Cauliflower, cut into florets	1	1	1

1 Place the garlic, coconut milk, coconut and curry powder in a pan, bring to the boil, then simmer for 15 minutes, stirring occasionally.

2 Remove from the heat and add the lemon juice, cayenne and a little salt and pepper.

3 Transfer to a dish and add the cauliflower, stirring to coat it well. Leave to marinate for 3–4 hours.

4 Thread the cauliflower on to soaked wooden skewers and barbecue for about 6 minutes until just cooked but still crisp.

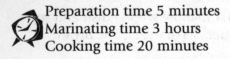
Preparation time 5 minutes
Marinating time 3 hours
Cooking time 20 minutes

Mixed Mushroom Kebabs

Serves 4

	METRIC	IMPERIAL	AMERICAN
Mixed, large mushrooms (chestnut, shiitake, oyster etc.)	450 g	1 lb	1 lb
Olive oil	120 ml	4 fl oz	½ cup
Salt and freshly ground black pepper			
Butter, melted	25 g	1 oz	2 tbsp
Garlic clove, crushed	1	1	1
Dry sherry	30 ml	2 tbsp	2 tbsp
Chopped fresh flat-leaf parsley	30 ml	2 tbsp	2 tbsp
To serve:			
Garlic bread (see page 121)			

1 Toss the mushrooms in the oil with plenty of pepper until the oil is absorbed.

2 Thread the mushrooms on to soaked wooden skewers.

3 Barbecue the kebabs for about 10 minutes, turning frequently until crispy.

4 Meanwhile, mix together the butter, garlic, sherry and parsley and season with salt and pepper.

5 Arrange the kebabs in a shallow serving dish and top with the flavoured butter. Serve with garlic bread.

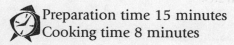
Preparation time 15 minutes
Cooking time 8 minutes

Parsnip and Pepper Kebabs

Serves 4

	METRIC	IMPERIAL	AMERICAN
Parsnips, cut into chunks	2	2	2
Red (bell) pepper, cut into squares	1	1	1
Yellow pepper, cut into squares	1	1	1
Green pepper, cut into squares	1	1	1
Shallots	8	8	8
Small courgettes (zucchini), cut into chunks	4	4	4
For the dressing:			
Soy sauce	60 ml	4 tbsp	4 tbsp
Oil	15 ml	1 tbsp	1 tbsp
Lemon juice	15 ml	1 tbsp	1 tbsp
Ground ginger	2.5 ml	½ tsp	½ tsp
Clear honey	30 ml	2 tbsp	2 tbsp

1 Blanch the parsnip and pepper squares in boiling water for 3 minutes, then drain.

2 Blanch the shallots in boiling water for about 5 minutes until just beginning to soften, then drain.

3 Blanch the courgettes in boiling water for 2 minutes, then drain.

4 Thread all the vegetables alternately on to soaked wooden skewers.

5 Mix together the dressing ingredients and brush well over the kebabs.

6 Barbecue the kebabs for about 10 minutes, turning and basting regularly as they cook.

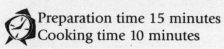Preparation time 15 minutes
Cooking time 10 minutes

Mushroom and Banana Kebabs

Serves 4

	METRIC	IMPERIAL	AMERICAN
Button mushrooms	225 g	8 oz	½ lb
Red (bell) peppers, cut into chunks	2	2	2
Large courgette (zucchini), cut into chunks	1	1	1
Firm banana, cut into chunks	1	1	1
Salt and freshly ground black pepper			
Freshly grated nutmeg			
Butter or margarine, melted	50 g	2 oz	¼ cup

1 Thread the vegetables and banana alternately on to soaked wooden skewers. Season with salt and pepper, sprinkle with nutmeg and brush well with butter or margarine.

2 Barbecue over a low heat for about 15 minutes, brushing and basting regularly, until the pepper and courgette chunks are tender.

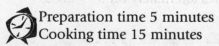Preparation time 5 minutes
Cooking time 15 minutes

Parsnip and Pears

Serves 4

	METRIC	IMPERIAL	AMERICAN
Parsnips, cut into chunks	350 g	12 oz	¾ lb
Salt			
Pears, peeled and quartered	4	4	4
Butter or margarine	50 g	2 oz	¼ cup
Light brown sugar	45 ml	3 tbsp	3 tbsp
Pinch of ground cinnamon			

1   Cook the parsnips in boiling salted water until just tender. Drain well.

2   Thread the parsnips and pears on to soaked wooden skewers.

3   Blend together the butter or margarine, sugar and cinnamon. Brush over the kebabs.

4   Barbecue for about 10 minutes, turning regularly and basting with more butter or margarine as they cook.

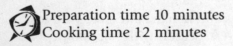
Preparation time 10 minutes
Cooking time 12 minutes

Colourful Kebabs

Serves 4

	METRIC	IMPERIAL	AMERICAN
Small aubergine (eggplant)	1	1	1
Courgette (zucchini)	1	1	1
Red (bell) pepper	1	1	1
Green pepper	1	1	1
Yellow or orange pepper	1	1	1
Shallots	4	4	4
Cherry tomatoes	8	8	8
Oil or butter			
Salt and freshly ground black pepper			

1 Cut the aubergine and courgette into slices. Cut the peppers into squares. Halve or quarter the shallots.

2 Thread all the vegetables including the tomatoes alternately on to soaked wooden skewers. Brush well with oil and season with salt and pepper.

3 Barbecue for about 10 minutes, turning frequently and brushing with more oil or butter as necessary.

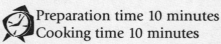 Preparation time 10 minutes
Cooking time 10 minutes

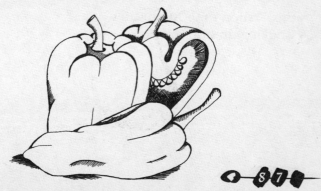

Tomato and Bread Kebabs

Serves 4

	METRIC	IMPERIAL	AMERICAN
White bread, unsliced and crusts removed	225 g	8 oz	½ lb
Cherry tomatoes	225 g	8 oz	½ lb
Garlic cloves, crushed	2	2	2
Olive oil	75 ml	5 tbsp	5 tbsp
Lemon juice	10 ml	2 tsp	2 tsp
Chopped fresh rosemary	15 ml	1 tbsp	1 tbsp
Chopped fresh thyme	15 ml	1 tbsp	1 tbsp
Salt and freshly ground black pepper			

1 Cut the bread into cubes about the same size as the tomatoes. Alternate the tomatoes and bread cubes on soaked wooden skewers.

2 Mix together the garlic, oil, lemon juice, herbs and a little salt and pepper. Brush generously over the kebabs.

3 Barbecue for about 10 minutes, turning frequently and brushing with more flavoured oil as they cook.

Preparation time 10 minutes
Cooking time 10 minutes

Spring Onions and Mushrooms with Soy Sauce

Serves 4

	METRIC	IMPERIAL	AMERICAN
Bunch of spring onions (scallions)	1	1	1
Button mushrooms	450 g	1 lb	1 lb
Lemon juice	60 ml	4 tbsp	4 tbsp
Soy sauce	30 ml	2 tbsp	2 tbsp
Oil	15 ml	1 tbsp	1 tbsp
Salt and freshly ground black pepper			

1 Cut the spring onions, green and white parts, into 2.5 cm/1 in pieces. Thread the spring onions and mushrooms alternately on soaked wooden skewers.

2 Whisk together the lemon juice, soy sauce, oil and a little salt and pepper. Brush over the kebabs.

3 Barbecue for 5 minutes, turning frequently and brushing with more flavoured oil as they cook.

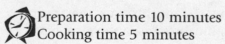
Preparation time 10 minutes
Cooking time 5 minutes

Garlic Vegetable Kebabs

Serves 4

	METRIC	IMPERIAL	AMERICAN
Small waxy potatoes, peeled but left whole	4	4	4
Shallots, peeled but left whole	4	4	4
Cup mushrooms	8	8	8
Small aubergine (eggplant), cut into 8 chunks	1	1	1
Bay leaves	4	4	4
Green (bell) pepper, cut into 8 chunks	1	1	1
Butter or margarine, melted	40 g	1½ oz	3 tbsp
Garlic clove, crushed	1	1	1
Salt and freshly ground black pepper			
Chopped fresh parsley	15 ml	1 tbsp	1 tbsp

1 Cook the potatoes and shallots separately in boiling, lightly salted water for about 5 minutes until almost tender. Drain.

2 Remove any stalks from the mushrooms, then thread the potatoes, shallots, mushrooms, aubergine, bay leaves and pepper chunks on soaked wooden skewers.

3 Mix the melted butter or margarine with the garlic, a little salt and pepper and the parsley.

4 Brush all over the kebabs, then barbecue for about 10 minutes until golden brown and cooked through, turning occasionally and brushing with the garlic butter.

5 Serve with any remaining garlic butter drizzled over.

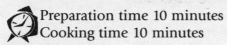Preparation time 10 minutes
Cooking time 10 minutes

Asparagus and Lemon Kebabs

Serves 4

	METRIC	IMPERIAL	AMERICAN
Quorn or smoked tofu	450 g	1 lb	2 cups
Asparagus spears, cut into chunks	225 g	8 oz	½ lb
Lemon, thinly sliced	1	1	1
Lemon juice	10 ml	2 tsp	2 tsp
Butter or margarine, melted	50 g	2 oz	¼ cup
Salt and freshly ground black pepper			

1 Thread the Quorn or tofu, asparagus and lemon slices alternately on to soaked wooden skewers. Sprinkle with lemon juice, brush with melted butter or margarine and season with salt and pepper.

2 Barbecue for about 10 minutes until cooked through and golden.

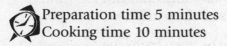Preparation time 5 minutes
Cooking time 10 minutes

Mediterranean Kebabs

Serves 4

	METRIC	IMPERIAL	AMERICAN
Jar of sun-dried tomatoes in oil	*285 g*	*10½ oz*	*1 small*
Courgettes (zucchini), thickly sliced	*4*	*4*	*4*
Chestnut mushrooms	*8*	*8*	*8*
Halloumi cheese, cut into 8 chunks	*100 g*	*4 oz*	*4 oz*
Dried oregano	*5 ml*	*1 tsp*	*1 tsp*
Ground cumin	*2.5 ml*	*½ tsp*	*½ tsp*
Red wine vinegar	*15 ml*	*1 tbsp*	*1 tbsp*
Garlic clove	*1*	*1*	*1*
Freshly ground black pepper			
Thin ciabatta loaf, cut lengthways into 4 slices	*1*	*1*	*1*

1 Drain the tomatoes, reserving the oil.

2 Blanch the courgettes in boiling, lightly salted water for 2 minutes. Drain, rinse with cold water and drain again.

3 Thread the tomatoes, courgettes, mushrooms and cheese on to soaked wooden skewers.

4 Mix 30 ml/2 tbsp of the tomato oil with the oregano, cumin, wine vinegar, garlic and lots of pepper. Brush over the kebabs and barbecue for about 10 minutes, turning frequently until golden (do not allow them to burn), and brushing with more of the basting mixture.

5 Brush any remaining basting mixture and tomato oil over the surfaces of the bread. Barbecue until lightly toasted. Place on plates and top with a kebab.

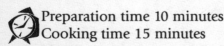
Preparation time 10 minutes
Cooking time 15 minutes

Golden Bites

Serves 4

	METRIC	IMPERIAL	AMERICAN
Corn on the cob, cut into 4 pieces	1	1	1
Yellow courgettes (zucchini), cut into 4 pieces	2	2	2
Yellow (bell) pepper, cut into 8 chunks	1	1	1
Small, unripe banana, cut into 4 pieces	1	1	1
Butter or margarine	40 g	1½ oz	3 tbsp
Grated fresh root ginger	5 ml	1 tsp	1 tsp
Pinch of turmeric			
Light soy sauce	5 ml	1 tsp	1 tsp
Grated rind and juice of ½ lemon			
Golden (light corn) syrup	10 ml	2 tsp	2 tsp
Salt and freshly ground black pepper			

1 Blanch all the vegetables (except the banana) in boiling, lightly salted water for 2 minutes. Drain.

2 Thread on to soaked wooden skewers with the banana.

3 Mix the remaining ingredients together and brush over the kebabs. Barbecue for about 10 minutes until golden and cooked through, turning occasionally and brushing liberally with the basting mixture. Serve with any extra mixture drizzled over.

 Preparation time 8 minutes
Cooking time 10 minutes

Vegetable Satay

Serves 4

	METRIC	IMPERIAL	AMERICAN
Small swede (rutabaga), cut into bite-sized chunks	1	1	1
Waxy baby new potatoes, scrubbed	8	8	8
Large carrots, cut into bite-sized chunks	2	2	2
Large courgettes (zucchini), cut into bite-sized chunks	2	2	2
Milk	75 ml	¼ pt	⅔ cup
Crunchy peanut butter	75 ml	5 tbsp	5 tbsp
Small green chilli, seeded and finely chopped	1	1	1
Butter or margarine	15 g	½ oz	1 tbsp
Clear honey	15 ml	1 tbsp	1 tbsp
Grated rind of ½ lime			

1 Boil the swede, potatoes and carrots until just tender in lightly salted water. Drain, rinse with cold water and drain again.

2 Blanch the courgettes in boiling, lightly salted water for 2 minutes. Drain, rinse with cold water and drain again.

3 Thread the vegetables on to soaked wooden skewers.

4 Warm the milk and peanut butter together with the chilli in a saucepan suitable for transferring to the barbecue, stirring until smooth. Keep warm at the side of the barbecue.

5 Melt the butter or margarine with the honey and grated lime rind.

6 Lay the kebabs on foil on the barbecue and brush with the melted mixture.

7 Barbecue until golden, turning and brushing with more basting mixture during cooking. Serve with the warm peanut sauce.

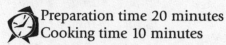

Preparation time 20 minutes
Cooking time 10 minutes

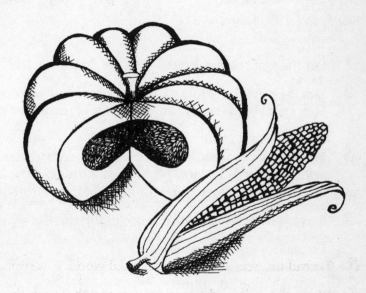

Quorn Teryaki

Serves 4

	METRIC	IMPERIAL	AMERICAN
Quorn chunks	200 g	7 oz	1¾ cups
Sunflower or groundnut (peanut) oil	30 ml	2 tbsp	2 tbsp
Soy sauce	60 ml	4 tbsp	4 tbsp
Sherry	15 ml	1 tbsp	1 tbsp
Light brown sugar	15 ml	1 tbsp	1 tbsp
Garlic clove, crushed	1	1	1
Grated fresh root ginger	5 ml	1 tsp	1 tsp
To serve:			
Plum sauce			

1   Put the Quorn chunks in a shallow dish.

2   Mix the remaining ingredients together and pour over. Toss gently and leave to marinate for at least 1 hour.

3   Thread on to soaked wooden skewers and barbecue until lightly golden and piping hot, turning frequently and brushing with more of the marinade.

4   Serve with a dish of plum sauce to dip in.

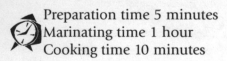

Preparation time 5 minutes
Marinating time 1 hour
Cooking time 10 minutes

FOIL PARCELS

Softer-textured vegetables cook very well on the barbecue in a parcel of foil, which seals in all the flavours and helps them blend together while cooking. Make larger parcels for convenience – and cook them for a little longer – or wrap the foods in individual portions for your guests to unwrap on their plates.

~~~~~~~~~~~~~~~~~

Italian-style Artichokes

Serves 4

	METRIC	IMPERIAL	AMERICAN
Can of artichoke hearts, drained	400 g	14 oz	1 large
White wine vinegar	15 ml	1 tbsp	1 tbsp
Chopped fresh basil	15 ml	1 tbsp	1 tbsp
Garlic clove, crushed	1	1	1
Parmesan cheese, freshly grated	100 g	4 oz	1 cup
Salt and freshly ground black pepper			

1 Thickly slice the artichokes and arrange them in four squares of foil, shiny side up. Sprinkle with vinegar, basil, garlic, cheese, salt and pepper.

2 Seal the parcels and barbecue for about 15 minutes until the vegetables have heated through.

Preparation time 10 minutes
Cooking time 15 minutes

Cheese Courgettes

Serves 4

	METRIC	IMPERIAL	AMERICAN
Courgettes (zucchini), thinly sliced	4	4	4
Garlic cloves, crushed	2	2	2
Olive oil	30 ml	2 tbsp	2 tbsp
Dried oregano	5 ml	1 tsp	1 tsp
Salt and freshly ground black pepper			
Emmenthal (Swiss) cheese, sliced	100 g	4 oz	¼ lb

1 Arrange the courgettes on four pieces of foil, shiny side up. Sprinkle with garlic and olive oil, then with oregano, salt and pepper.

2 Arrange the cheese on top.

3 Seal the parcels and barbecue for about 15 minutes until the courgettes are tender and the cheese has melted.

Preparation time 10 minutes
Cooking time 15 minutes

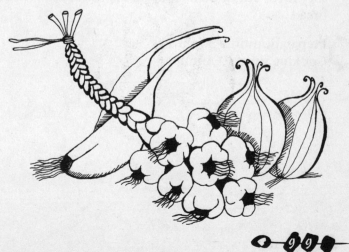

Roasted Garlic

Serves 4

	METRIC	IMPERIAL	AMERICAN
Garlic bulbs	4	4	4
Oil	60 ml	4 tbsp	4 tbsp
Butter or margarine	40 g	1½ oz	3 tbsp
Chopped fresh oregano	30 ml	2 tbsp	2 tbsp
To serve:			
French bread			

1 Leave the garlic bulbs unpeeled. Slice off the tops to expose the cloves inside the skins. Place each one on a piece of foil, shiny side up, drizzle with oil and dot with butter or margarine, then sprinkle with oregano.

2 Close the foil parcels and place on the side of the barbecue for about 40 minutes, opening the parcels to baste once during cooking with the flavoured oil and butter.

3 To serve, remove the garlic from the parcels, squeeze the cloves out of their skins and spread over French bread.

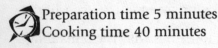
Preparation time 5 minutes
Cooking time 40 minutes

Chestnut Mushroom Parcels

Serves 4

	METRIC	IMPERIAL	AMERICAN
Chestnut mushrooms, sliced	450 g	1 lb	1 lb
Spring onions (scallions), chopped	2	2	2
Garlic cloves, crushed	2	2	2
Olive oil	60 ml	4 tbsp	4 tbsp
Balsamic vinegar	15 ml	1 tbsp	1 tbsp
Chopped fresh parsley	15 ml	1 tbsp	1 tbsp
Salt and freshly ground black pepper			
Tomatoes, halved	4	4	4
Chopped fresh basil	15 ml	1 tbsp	1 tbsp

1 Place the mushrooms in four squares of foil, shiny side up. Sprinkle with spring onions and garlic.

2 Whisk together 45 ml/3 tbsp of the oil with the vinegar, stir in the parsley and season with salt and pepper. Pour over the mushroom parcels and twist the foil at the top to seal.

3 Barbecue for about 20 minutes until cooked through.

4 Meanwhile, brush the tomatoes with the remaining oil, season with salt and pepper and barbecue for about 5 minutes until cooked.

5 Serve sprinkled with chopped basil.

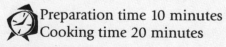 Preparation time 10 minutes
Cooking time 20 minutes

Mixed Vegetable Parcels

Serves 4

	METRIC	IMPERIAL	AMERICAN
Small aubergine (eggplant), sliced	1	1	1
Small courgette (zucchini), sliced	1	1	1
Red (bell) pepper, sliced	1	1	1
Green pepper, sliced	1	1	1
Button mushrooms, sliced	100 g	4 oz	¼ lb
Shallots, sliced	2	2	2
Cherry tomatoes	4	4	4
Garlic cloves, crushed	2	2	2
Olive oil	45 ml	3 tbsp	3 tbsp
Chopped fresh thyme	10 ml	2 tsp	2 tsp
Salt and freshly ground black pepper			

1 Prepare all the vegetables and divide them between four pieces of foil, shiny side up. Sprinkle with crushed garlic, oil, thyme, salt and pepper. Seal the foil parcels.

2 Barbecue for about 25 minutes until the vegetables are tender.

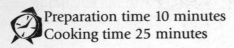
Preparation time 10 minutes
Cooking time 25 minutes

Marinated Pecans

Serves 4

	METRIC	IMPERIAL	AMERICAN
Pecan halves	225 g	8 oz	2 cups
Orange juice	90 ml	6 tbsp	6 tbsp
Curry powder	10 ml	2 tsp	2 tsp
Vegetarian Worcestershire sauce	10 ml	2 tsp	2 tsp
Light brown sugar	5 ml	1 tsp	1 tsp
Garlic clove, crushed	1	1	1
Salt and freshly ground black pepper			

1 Mix together all the ingredients in a bowl and leave to stand for at least 1 hour.

2 Drain the nuts and divide them between four pieces of foil, shiny side up.

3 Seal the parcels and barbecue the nuts at the side of the barbecue for about 1 hour.

Preparation time 5 minutes
Marinating time 1 hour
Cooking time 1 hour

Warm Italian Salad Parcels

Serves 4

	METRIC	IMPERIAL	AMERICAN
Cucumber, thinly sliced	¹/₂	¹/₂	¹/₂
Plum tomatoes, thinly sliced	4	4	4
Red onion, thinly sliced	1	1	1
Black olives, stoned (pitted) and halved	8	8	8
A handful of fresh basil leaves			
Olive oil			
White wine vinegar			
Salt and freshly ground black pepper			

1 Place the cucumber, tomatoes and onion rings in a thin layer on four pieces of foil, shiny side up.

2 Scatter with the olives and tuck in a basil leaf here and there.

3 Drizzle with a little olive oil and a sprinkling of wine vinegar. Season with a very little salt and a good grinding of black pepper.

4 Seal the parcels. Barbecue for 2–3 minutes until warmed through but still with lots of texture. Serve straight away.

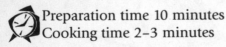
Preparation time 10 minutes
Cooking time 2–3 minutes

Chilli-stuffed Peppers

Serves 4

	METRIC	IMPERIAL	AMERICAN
Green or red (bell) peppers	4	4	4
Cheddar cheese, grated	75 g	3 oz	¾ cup
Mushrooms, finely chopped	50 g	2 oz	½ cup
Can of red kidney beans, drained	425 g	15 oz	1 large
Tomato chilli salsa (ready-made)	60 ml	4 tbsp	4 tbsp
Ground cumin	2.5 ml	½ tsp	½ tsp
Dried oregano	5 ml	1 tsp	1 tsp
Garlic salt			
Freshly ground black pepper			

1   Cut a slice off the top of each pepper and remove the seeds. Boil the peppers and lids in lightly salted water for 6 minutes until just tender. Drain, rinse with cold water and drain again. Dry on kitchen paper.

2   Mix 50 g/2 oz/½ cup of the cheese with the remaining ingredients and spoon into the peppers. Top with the remaining cheese, then the 'lids'.

3   Place on four pieces of foil, shiny side up. Seal the parcels. Barbecue for about 30 minutes, turning occasionally, until piping hot and cooked through.

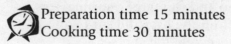

Preparation time 15 minutes
Cooking time 30 minutes

Nutty-stuffed Mushrooms

Serves 4

	METRIC	IMPERIAL	AMERICAN
Large flat mushrooms, peeled	4	4	4
Butter or margarine	50 g	2 oz	¼ cup
Spring onions (scallions), finely chopped	2	2	2
Hazelnuts, chopped	50 g	2 oz	½ cup
Soy sauce	10 ml	2 tsp	2 tsp
Dry white wine	15 ml	1 tbsp	1 tbsp
Garlic clove, crushed	1	1	1
Fresh breadcrumbs	25 g	1 oz	½ cup
Salt and freshly ground black pepper			
Dried thyme	2.5 ml	½ tsp	½ tsp
Mozzarella cheese, grated	50 g	2 oz	½ cup

1 Remove the mushroom stalks and chop finely.

2 Melt the butter or margarine in a saucepan and use a little to brush over four squares of foil, shiny side up. Put a mushroom gill-side up on each piece of foil.

3 Add the spring onions and chopped mushroom stalks to the saucepan and fry (sauté), stirring, for 2 minutes. Remove from the heat and stir in all the remaining ingredients except the cheese.

4 Pile on to the mushrooms and press firmly in place. Seal the parcels and barbecue for 4 minutes, stuffing-side down, then turn over and continue cooking for a further 4–6 minutes.

5 Open the foil, sprinkle with the cheese and cook for a few minutes until the cheese melts. Serve straight away.

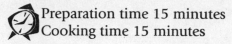
Preparation time 15 minutes
Cooking time 15 minutes

Herby Potato Parcels

Serves 4

	METRIC	IMPERIAL	AMERICAN
Butter or margarine	50 g	2 oz	¼ cup
Potatoes, scrubbed and thinly sliced	4	4	4
Chopped fresh parsley	15 ml	1 tbsp	1 tbsp
Snipped fresh chives	15 ml	1 tbsp	1 tbsp
Chopped fresh sage	5 ml	1 tsp	1 tsp
Salt and freshly ground black pepper			

1 Melt the butter or margarine in a large saucepan. Remove from the heat.

2 Add the sliced potatoes, herbs and a little salt and pepper and toss until each slice is coated.

3 Divide in a thin, even layer on four pieces of foil, shiny side up. Seal the parcels and barbecue for about 20 minutes, turning occasionally, until the potato is tender.

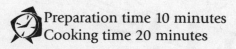
Preparation time 10 minutes
Cooking time 20 minutes

Minted New Potato Parcels

Serves 4

	METRIC	IMPERIAL	AMERICAN
Butter or margarine, melted	25 g	1 oz	2 tbsp
Small new potatoes, washed	16	16	16
Chopped fresh mint	20 ml	4 tsp	4 tsp
Salt and freshly ground black pepper			

1 Brush the shiny side of four pieces of foil with a little of the melted butter or margarine. Top each with four potatoes.

2 Sprinkle with mint and a little salt and pepper and drizzle with the remaining melted fat.

3 Seal the parcels and barbecue directly on the hot coals for about 20–30 minutes until the potatoes are tender.

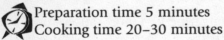

Preparation time 5 minutes
Cooking time 20–30 minutes

Potatoes with Edam, Onion and Basil

Serves 4

	METRIC	IMPERIAL	AMERICAN
Medium potatoes, scrubbed	4	4	4
Onions, thinly sliced	2	2	2
Butter or margarine	25 g	1 oz	2 tbsp
Edam cheese, grated	100 g	4 oz	¼ lb
Fresh basil leaves	16	16	16
Salt and freshly ground black pepper			

1 Boil the potatoes in their skins until just tender. Drain.

2 When cold enough to handle, cut into five thick slices, not quite right through the base, and place on four squares of greased foil.

3 Meanwhile, fry (sauté) the onions in the butter or margarine for 2 minutes to soften.

4 Push the onions in between each slice of potato with a basil leaf and some cheese. Season with salt and pepper.

5 Seal the parcels and barbecue for about 15–20 minutes, turning occasionally, until piping hot and the cheese has melted.

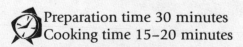
Preparation time 30 minutes
Cooking time 15–20 minutes

Grilled Baby Squash with Cheese and Chives

Courgettes (zucchini) make a good alternative to the baby squash if you prefer.

Serves 4

	METRIC	IMPERIAL	AMERICAN
Baby squash	4	4	4
Salt and freshly ground black pepper			
Cheddar cheese, grated	75 g	3 oz	¾ cup
Snipped fresh chives	30 ml	2 tbsp	2 tbsp
Butter or margarine	25 g	1 oz	2 tbsp

1   Cut the squash in halves and scoop out the seeds (pits). Season the flesh lightly.

2   Mash the cheese, chives, butter or margarine and a little salt and pepper together and spoon into the cavities in the squash.

3   Put the two halves of each squash back together again, encasing the cheese mixture. Place on four squares of foil, shiny side up. Seal the parcels.

4   Barbecue for about 20 minutes, turning frequently until the flesh is tender. Let the guests open the parcels on their plates.

Preparation time 10 minutes
Cooking time 20 minutes

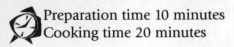

Creamy Garlic Mushrooms

Serves 4

	METRIC	IMPERIAL	AMERICAN
Large flat mushrooms	8	8	8
Butter or margarine, melted	25 g	1 oz	2 tbsp
Garlic cloves, finely chopped	2	2	2
Chopped fresh parsley	30 ml	2 tbsp	2 tbsp
White wine	60 ml	4 tbsp	4 tbsp
Double (heavy) cream	60 ml	4 tbsp	4 tbsp
Salt and freshly ground black pepper			

1   Peel the mushrooms and remove any stalks. Chop the stalks and scatter over the gills of the mushrooms.

2   Butter four large pieces of foil and lay two mushrooms on each. Scatter over the garlic and parsley.

3   Blend the wine and cream together and spoon over. Season well.

4   Seal the parcels and barbecue for about 10–15 minutes until the mushrooms are tender.

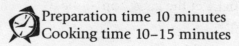
Preparation time 10 minutes
Cooking time 10–15 minutes

INTERESTING EXTRAS

You need some side dishes to go with your barbecued foods, and it is usually best to prepare these in the kitchen and have them ready to serve when the main course from the barbecue is cooking and piping hot. Here is a selection of simple vegetable, rice and grain dishes and bread ideas that offer interesting barbecue combinations.

You can also use your conventional oven to keep foods warm, especially if you have a large number of guests and a relatively small barbecue. Preheat the oven to 160°C/325°F/gas mark 3 to make sure that dishes stay hot without overcooking, but do keep an eye on the foods to make sure they are still at their best. Place them on ovenproof serving plates and cover tightly with foil to retain the moisture before placing in the oven. Don't leave them there longer than you have to.

Artichoke Cream

Serves 4

	METRIC	IMPERIAL	AMERICAN
Can of artichoke hearts, drained	400 g	14 oz	1 large
Mayonnaise (see page 138)	250 ml	8 fl oz	1 cup
Garlic clove, crushed	1	1	1
Chopped fresh basil	5 ml	1 tsp	1 tsp
White wine vinegar	5 ml	1 tsp	1 tsp
Salt and freshly ground black pepper			
Parmesan cheese, grated	75 g	3 oz	³/₄ cup
Fresh breadcrumbs	25 g	1 oz	¹/₂ cup

1 Arrange the artichokes in a shallow ovenproof dish.

2 Mix together the mayonnaise, garlic, basil, vinegar, salt and pepper and pour over the artichokes.

3 Mix together the cheese and breadcrumbs and sprinkle over the top.

4 Bake in the oven at 200°C/400°F/gas mark 6 for 20–25 minutes until golden.

 Preparation time 5 minutes
Cooking time 25 minutes

Celery and Beans in Soured Cream

Serves 4

	METRIC	IMPERIAL	AMERICAN
Celery sticks	6	6	6
French (green) beans, trimmed	450 g	1 lb	1 lb
Olive oil	60 ml	4 tbsp	4 tbsp
Soured (dairy sour) cream	150 ml	¼ pt	⅔ cup
Caraway seeds	15 ml	1 tbsp	1 tbsp
Salt and freshly ground black pepper			

1   Cut the celery into pieces the same size as the beans.

2   Cook the celery in boiling water for 6 minutes, adding the beans for the last 2 minutes, then drain well.

3   Heat the oil and fry (sauté) the vegetables quickly for 2 minutes.

4   Stir in the soured cream and caraway seeds and season with salt and pepper.

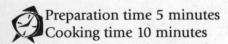

Preparation time 5 minutes
Cooking time 10 minutes

Sweet Glazed Shallots

Serves 4-6

	METRIC	IMPERIAL	AMERICAN
Small shallots	450 g	1 lb	1 lb
Butter or margarine, melted	50 g	2 oz	¼ cup
Golden (light corn) syrup	60 ml	4 tbsp	4 tbsp

1 Peel the shallots, then place them in a pan, cover with water and bring to the boil. Simmer for 4 minutes, then drain thoroughly.

2 Arrange the shallots in a shallow baking tin (pan) and pour over the butter or margarine. Drizzle with the syrup.

3 Cook in a preheated oven at 200°C/400°F/gas mark 6 for about 20 minutes, stirring occasionally, until the shallots are tender and golden.

Preparation time 5 minutes
Cooking time 25 minutes

Mushrooms in Balsamic Vinegar

Serves 4

	METRIC	IMPERIAL	AMERICAN
Button mushrooms	450 g	1 lb	1 lb
Lemon juice	30 ml	2 tbsp	2 tbsp
Salt and freshly ground black pepper			
Balsamic vinegar	150 ml	¼ pt	⅔ cup
Olive oil	120 ml	4 fl oz	½ cup
Garlic cloves, crushed	4	4	4
Chopped capers	15 ml	1 tbsp	1 tbsp
Chopped fresh parsley	45 ml	3 tbsp	3 tbsp

1 Place the mushrooms and lemon juice in a pan and season with salt and pepper. Add just enough water to cover, bring to the boil, then simmer for about 5 minutes until tender. Drain.

2 Meanwhile, bring the vinegar, oil and garlic to the boil in a separate pan. Simmer for 20 minutes.

3 Pour this hot marinade over the mushrooms, then leave to cool.

4 Add the capers and parsley and season with salt and pepper.

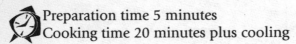
Preparation time 5 minutes
Cooking time 20 minutes plus cooling

Potato Ideas

* Pre-cook jacket potatoes to save time. Pierce scrubbed potatoes with a fork and microwave on high for about 3 minutes per potato. Rub with a little coarse salt and oil, then wrap in foil. Alternatively, season and wrap them and cook them in a hot oven at 200°C/400°F/gas mark 6 for about 1 hour. Place the wrapped potatoes directly on the barbecue coals to finish cooking.

* Offer a selection of toppings for baked potatoes: grated or crumbled cheese; pats of herb butter (see page 32); pats of garlic butter – as strong as you dare! (see page 32); fresh tomato sauce (see page 26); even hot baked beans.

* Peel and slice potatoes and layer in an ovenproof dish, sprinkling with salt, pepper and your favourite herb as you go. Half-fill the dish with milk, dot with butter and bake in a preheated oven at 200°C/400°F/gas mark 6 for about 50 minutes until tender and the top is browned.

* Peel potatoes and slice thickly, without cutting right through to the base (much as you would to make garlic bread). Slide a piece of bay leaf into each slit, sprinkle with salt and pepper and brush with plenty of olive oil. Bake in a preheated oven at 190°C/375°F/gas mark 5 for about 1 hour, depending on size, until they are tender and golden.

Wild Rice Salad

Serves 4

	METRIC	IMPERIAL	AMERICAN
Vegetable stock	450 ml	¾ pt	2 cups
Wild rice	100 g	4 oz	½ cup
Long-grain rice	175 g	6 oz	¾ cup
Can of red pimientos, drained and chopped	400 g	14 oz	1 large
Oil	60 ml	4 tbsp	4 tbsp
Red wine vinegar	30 ml	2 tbsp	2 tbsp
Vegetarian Worcestershire sauce	5 ml	1 tsp	1 tsp
Salt and freshly ground black pepper			

1 Bring the stock to the boil. Pour in the wild rice, return to the boil, cover and simmer gently for 35 minutes.

2 Add the long-grain rice, cover again and simmer for about 10–15 minutes until all the rice is cooked.

3 If there is any liquid left, uncover and boil until absorbed. Leave to cool.

4 Stir in the pimientos.

5 Mix together the oil, vinegar, Worcestershire sauce, and a little salt and pepper. Pour over the rice mixture and toss together well.

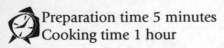
Preparation time 5 minutes
Cooking time 1 hour

Rice Ideas

* Rice can be used hot or cold, as the basis for a warming accompaniment, or an interesting salad.

* To save time when your guests are arriving or your family is hungry, cook long-grain rice in advance and drain it well. You can then use it for a quick fried-rice dish, either cooked conventionally or in a frying pan (skillet) on the barbecue, or to make a rice salad.

* To make ginger and pepper fried rice: heat a little olive oil and gently soften some chopped onion, garlic and red and green (bell) pepper. Stir in some cooked long-grain rice and 5 ml/1 tsp minced ginger and stir together until hot. Season with salt and pepper or soy sauce.

* If you are serving Eastern-inspired barbecued foods, choose a Chinese fried-rice dish.

* If you like a simple side dish, cook rice in a vegetable stock to give it extra flavour.

* Add a finely pared lemon rind to the water when cooking rice, then sprinkle it with a little lemon juice and top with 5 ml/1 tsp grated lemon rind to serve.

Spiced Bulghar with Pine Nuts

Serves 4

	METRIC	IMPERIAL	AMERICAN
Olive oil	60 ml	4 tbsp	4 tbsp
Onions, finely chopped	225 g	8 oz	½ lb
Garlic clove, finely chopped	1	1	1
Pine nuts	30 ml	2 tbsp	2 tbsp
Bulghar wheat	150 g	5 oz	scant 1 cup
Vegetable stock	600 ml	1 pt	2½ cups
Salt and freshly ground black pepper			
Raisins	30 ml	2 tbsp	2 tbsp
Pinch of ground coriander (cilantro)			
Pinch of ground cinnamon			

1 Heat half the oil and gently fry (sauté) the onions until beginning to soften.

2 Add the garlic and pine nuts and continue to fry until the onions are soft.

3 Stir in the bulghar and the remaining oil and mix well together. Add the stock and the remaining ingredients, cover and bring to the boil.

4 Simmer for about 15 minutes until all the stock is absorbed.

5 If serving hot, stand the pan in a warm place or at the side of the barbecue for about 30 minutes until the bulghar is soft and swollen.

6 Fluff up with a fork before serving hot or cold.

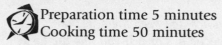
Preparation time 5 minutes
Cooking time 50 minutes

Garlic Bread

Adding parsley to the garlic butter reduces the pungency of the garlic on the breath. The amount of garlic you use is very much a matter of personal taste.

Serves 4

	METRIC	IMPERIAL	AMERICAN
Garlic cloves, crushed	2	2	2
Butter or margarine, softened	100 g	4 oz	½ cup
A few drops of lemon juice			
Chopped fresh parsley	15 ml	1 tbsp	1 tbsp
French stick	1	1	1

1 Blend together the garlic, butter or margarine, lemon juice and parsley.

2 Cut the bread in diagonal slices about 2 cm/¾ in thick without cutting right through the base.

3 Spread all the cut sides of the bread with the garlic butter, then wrap the bread in foil.

4 Place the bread in the oven at 200°C/400°F/gas mark 6 for about 20 minutes, or place at the side of the barbecue until the butter has melted into the bread and it is hot and crisp on the edges.

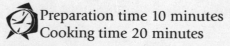
Preparation time 10 minutes
Cooking time 20 minutes

Vegetable Pitta Packets

Make and wrap these in advance and keep them in the warming drawer if your barbecue has one. If you like the taste of ginger but can't be bothered with fresh, buy a jar of minced ginger to keep in the fridge.

Serves 4

	METRIC	IMPERIAL	AMERICAN
Vegetable stock	300 ml	½ pt	1¼ cups
Leeks, sliced	225 g	8 oz	½ lb
Small apple, chopped	1	1	1
Radishes, chopped	6	6	6
Button mushrooms, sliced	4	4	4
Grated fresh root ginger	10 ml	2 tsp	2 tsp
Salt and freshly ground black pepper			
Olive oil	60 ml	4 tbsp	4 tbsp
White wine vinegar	15 ml	1 tbsp	1 tbsp
Pinch of mustard powder			
Pitta breads	4	4	4

1   Bring the stock to the boil in a pan, add the leeks and simmer for about 10 minutes until soft. Drain and cool.

2   Mix together the leeks, apple, radishes, mushrooms and ginger. Season with salt and pepper.

3   Blend together 45 ml/3 tbsp of the oil, the wine vinegar and mustard powder and sprinkle over the vegetables.

4 Slit the pitta breads lengthways down one side and fill with the vegetable mixture. Brush the outsides with the remaining oil and wrap the breads individually in foil.

5 Heat on the barbecue for about 6 minutes.

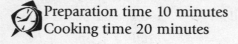
Preparation time 10 minutes
Cooking time 20 minutes

Classic Campfire Damper

Serves 4

	METRIC	IMPERIAL	AMERICAN
Self-raising (self-rising) flour	350 g	12 oz	3 cups
Salt	5 ml	1 tsp	1 tsp
Dried milk (non-fat milk powder)	15 ml	1 tbsp	1 tbsp
Butter or margarine	25 g	1 oz	2 tbsp
Water	300 ml	½ pt	1¼ cups

A little extra butter or margarine for greasing
   and flour for dusting

1 Mix the flour and salt with the dried milk.

2 Rub in the butter or margarine.

3 Quickly mix in the water with a knife until the
   mixture forms a dough. Knead in the bowl for a few
   minutes until smooth.

4 Shape into a round and place on a piece of greased
   and floured foil, shiny side up.

5 Make a few slashes in the top with a knife, then wrap
   loosely but securely in foil. Place in the hot coals and
   cook for about 20 minutes until golden brown and
   the base sounds hollow when tapped. Serve hot.

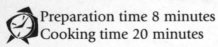
Preparation time 8 minutes
Cooking time 20 minutes

Bread Ideas

When you are in a hurry, the last thing you are likely to think about is making bread – especially when there are no end of interesting ones available in the supermarkets and bakers; we are almost spoilt for choice. Two or three tasty breads served with a barbecue add variety and interest.

* French baguettes are great – but there are lots of other possibilities. Try some of the Mediterranean-style breads with olives or sun-dried tomatoes, Italian breads such as ciabatta or pugili, or warm pitta breads. Most of these freeze well, so you can keep something in the freezer for when you need it.

* Wrap the bread in foil and warm it at the side of the barbecue to add that wonderful aroma of warm bread to the cooking.

* Rub a cut garlic clove over slices of baguette or crusty bread, then rub with the cut side of a ripe tomato (or with a tinned tomato) and sprinkle generously with olive oil, salt and freshly ground black pepper. Serve as a starter or with the meal.

* Don't forget melba toasts or any of the vast range of interesting crackers you can buy to serve as a side dish or if you are serving dips.

* If all you have is some stale bread, don't despair. Cut it thinly and toast it, then cut it into fingers to make your own crisp melba toasts. Or cut it into squares or triangles and fry (sauté) in hot oil with a dried chilli to make delicious croûtons.

SALADS AND SALAD DRESSINGS

The crisp, fresh taste of a salad is the perfect complement for barbecued foods, so be imaginative and serve two or three different ones. There's a great selection here.

〰〰〰〰〰〰〰

Hot Lentil Salad

Serves 4

	METRIC	IMPERIAL	AMERICAN
Can of green or brown lentils, drained	400 g	14 oz	1 large
Oil	45 ml	3 tbsp	3 tbsp
Button mushrooms, sliced	100 g	4 oz	¼ lb
Red wine vinegar	45 m	3 tbsp	3 tbsp
Mild mustard	5 ml	1 tsp	1 tsp
Salt and freshly ground black pepper			
Chopped fresh parsley	15 ml	1 tbsp	1 tbsp

1 Warm the lentils gently in a pan.

2 Meanwhile, heat a little of the oil and fry (sauté) the mushrooms for 3 minutes.

3 Blend the remaining oil with the wine vinegar, mustard and a little salt and pepper to make a vinaigrette.

4 Drain the lentils, mix with the mushrooms and blend with the dressing. Season again with salt and pepper to taste. Sprinkle with parsley and serve hot.

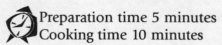
Preparation time 5 minutes
Cooking time 10 minutes

Sun-dried Tomato and Artichoke Salad

Serves 4

	METRIC	IMPERIAL	AMERICAN
Can of artichoke hearts, drained	400 g	14 oz	1 large
Sun-dried tomatoes	8	8	8
Black olives, stoned (pitted)	12	12	12
Pine nuts, toasted	45 ml	3 tbsp	3 tbsp
Chopped fresh basil	30 ml	2 tbsp	2 tbsp
Lemon juice	90 ml	6 tbsp	6 tbsp
Olive oil	60 ml	4 tbsp	4 tbsp
Salt and freshly ground black pepper			

1 Cut the artichoke hearts into quarters and place in a bowl.

2 Cut the tomatoes into julienne strips and add to the artichokes with the olives, pine nuts and basil.

3 Blend together the lemon juice and olive oil and season with salt and pepper.

4 Pour over the salad and toss well.

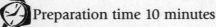 Preparation time 10 minutes

Crispy Fruit Coleslaw

Serves 4

	METRIC	IMPERIAL	AMERICAN
Small white cabbage	½	½	½
Small onion, grated	1	1	1
Carrot, grated	1	1	1
Eating (dessert) apple, grated	1	1	1
Raisins or sultanas (golden raisins)	50 g	2 oz	⅓ cup
Mayonnaise (see page 138)	150 ml	¼ pt	⅔ cup
A little milk			
Salt and freshly ground black pepper			

1 Shred the cabbage finely and place in a large bowl.

2 Add the onion, carrot, apple and raisins or sultanas and mix well.

3 Thin the mayonnaise with a little milk and season with salt and pepper. Pour over the salad and toss together well.

 Preparation time 15 minutes

Aubergine Salad

Serves 4

	METRIC	IMPERIAL	AMERICAN
Tomatoes, cut into small wedges	2	2	2
Red (bell) pepper, cut into strips	1	1	1
Onion, cut into rings	1	1	1
White wine vinegar	30 ml	2 tbsp	2 tbsp
Dry sherry	30 ml	2 tbsp	2 tbsp
Oil	90 ml	6 tbsp	6 tbsp
Sesame oil	5 ml	1 tsp	1 tsp
Pinch of sugar			
Salt and freshly ground black pepper			
Aubergine (eggplant)	1	1	1
Lemon juice	30 ml	2 tbsp	2 tbsp

1   Mix the tomatoes, pepper and onion in a salad bowl.

2   Mix together the vinegar, sherry, 15 ml/1 tbsp of the oil, the sesame oil, sugar and a little salt and pepper. Pour over the salad and leave to marinate.

3   Cut the aubergine into thin strips and toss in lemon juice to prevent discolouring.

4   Heat the remaining oil and fry (sauté) the aubergine for about 8 minutes until lightly browned. Drain well and leave to cool.

5   Mix the aubergine into the salad and toss together gently.

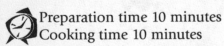
Preparation time 10 minutes
Cooking time 10 minutes

Colourful Salad

Serves 4

	METRIC	IMPERIAL	AMERICAN
Green (bell) pepper, cut into strips	1	1	1
Hard-boiled (hard-cooked) eggs, quartered	2	2	2
Cucumber, thinly sliced	5 cm	2 in	2 in
Tomatoes, cut into wedges	2	2	2
Black olives, stoned (pitted)	8	8	8
Green olives, stoned	8	8	8
Capers	5 ml	1 tsp	1 tsp
Vinaigrette (see page 139)	45 ml	3 tbsp	3 tbsp
Salt and freshly ground black pepper			

1 Place all the salad ingredients in a bowl and pour over the vinaigrette.

2 Toss together gently, then season with salt and pepper.

 Preparation time 5 minutes

Red Cabbage Salad

Always toss apples in a little lemon juice as soon as you have sliced them to prevent them from going brown.

Serves 4

	METRIC	IMPERIAL	AMERICAN
Red cabbage, finely shredded	225 g	8 oz	½ lb
Orange, peeled and cut into chunks	1	1	1
Eating (dessert) apple, cut into chunks	1	1	1
Sultanas (golden raisins)	50 g	2 oz	⅓ cup
Orange juice	60 ml	4 tbsp	4 tbsp
Lemon juice	15 ml	1 tbsp	1 tbsp
Clear honey	15 ml	1 tbsp	1 tbsp
Oil	60 ml	4 tbsp	4 tbsp
Salt and freshly ground black pepper			
Banana	1	1	1

1 Mix together the cabbage, orange, apple and sultanas in a salad bowl.

2 Whisk together the orange and lemon juice, honey and oil. Season with salt and pepper.

3 Pour over the salad and toss together well. Leave to stand for 2 hours.

4 Just before serving, slice the banana and add it to the salad. Toss again and adjust the seasoning to taste.

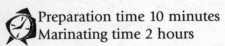
Preparation time 10 minutes
Marinating time 2 hours

Greek Potato Salad

Serves 4

	METRIC	IMPERIAL	AMERICAN
New potatoes, cooked and diced	450 g	1 lb	1 lb
Tomatoes, chopped	225 g	8 oz	½ lb
Onion, finely chopped	1	1	1
Black olives, stoned (pitted)	50 g	2 oz	⅓ cup
Mayonnaise (see page 138)	45 ml	3 tbsp	3 tbsp
Plain yoghurt	30 ml	2 tbsp	2 tbsp
Salt and freshly ground black pepper			

1 Carefully mix together the potatoes, tomatoes, onion and olives.

2 Mix together the mayonnaise and yoghurt and season with salt and pepper.

3 Pour the dressing over the salad and toss well. Chill before serving.

 Preparation time 10 minutes plus chilling

Cucumber and Walnut Salad

Serves 4

	METRIC	IMPERIAL	AMERICAN
Cucumber, sliced	350 g	12 oz	³/₄ lb
Radishes, thinly sliced	8	8	8
Green (bell) pepper, chopped	1	1	1
Spring onions (scallions), chopped	2	2	2
Walnuts, chopped	50 g	2 oz	¹/₂ cup
Chopped fresh parsley	15 ml	1 tbsp	1 tbsp
Chopped fresh thyme	5 ml	1 tsp	1 tsp
For the dressing:			
Soy sauce	60 ml	4 tbsp	4 tbsp
Oil	15 ml	1 tbsp	1 tbsp
Lemon juice	15 ml	1 tbsp	1 tbsp
Ground ginger	2.5 ml	¹/₂ tsp	¹/₂ tsp
Clear honey, warmed	15 ml	1 tbsp	1 tbsp
Water	60 ml	4 tbsp	4 tbsp

1 Mix together all the salad ingredients.

2 Whisk together the dressing ingredients.

3 Pour the dressing over the salad and toss together well.

Preparation time 10 minutes

Feta and Cucumber Salad

Serves 4

	METRIC	IMPERIAL	AMERICAN
Cucumber	1	1	1
Feta cheese, crumbled	225 g	8 oz	2 cups
Chopped fresh mint	45 ml	3 tbsp	3 tbsp
Caster (superfine) sugar	15 ml	1 tbsp	1 tbsp
Olive oil	90 ml	6 tbsp	6 tbsp
White wine vinegar	45 ml	3 tbsp	3 tbsp
Salt and freshly ground black pepper			

1 Slice the cucumber very thinly, using a mandoline if possible. Arrange in a shallow serving dish and sprinkle with the cheese and mint. Sprinkle over the sugar.

2 Whisk together the oil and vinegar and season with salt and pepper.

3 Pour over the salad and leave to stand for 1 hour before serving.

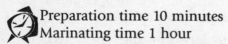
Preparation time 10 minutes
Marinating time 1 hour

Salad Ideas

* Coarsely grate four or five carrots and season with lots of freshly ground black pepper, then dress in a simple vinaigrette dressing (see page 139), or with 45 ml/ 3 tbsp orange juice mixed with 15 ml/1 tbsp lemon juice; or with a yoghurt or fromage frais dressing (see page 47).

* Layer sliced tomatoes with a sprinkling of sugar and snipped fresh chives, then spoon over some vinaigrette dressing (see page 139). Leave for an hour before serving, if you can.

* Dress a rinsed and drained can of mixed pulses with vinaigrette dressing (see page 139) and sprinkle with fresh herbs.

* Mix cooked long-grain rice (about 100 g/4 oz/½ cup uncooked rice serves four) with a selection of: chopped onion or spring onion (scallion), cooked peas, chopped mushrooms, then drizzle with vinaigrette (see page 139) or blend a little curry powder into 45ml/3 tbsp mayonnaise (see page 138) and stir gently into the rice salad.

* Cook small pasta shapes in vegetable stock instead of water, then drain well. Mix with diced canned pimientos, season well with salt and pepper and dress with a little vinaigrette (see page 139).

* Don't just automatically buy the same type of iceberg or round lettuce; there's loads more choice on the supermarket or greengrocers' shelves. Go for a contrast in flavours and textures; risk an unusual combination. You can choose from: little gem, lambs' lettuce, oakleaf, lollo rosso, lollo biondo, dandelion, spinach leaves, cos (romaine), Chinese leaves (stem lettuce), curly endive (chicory) – the variety is almost endless!

❋ Make a basic potato salad of boiled new or chopped potatoes with mayonnaise (see page 138), add some chopped spring onions (scallions); freshly snipped chives; and/or a spoonful of soured (dairy sour) cream.

❋ Mix drained, diced cucumber into Greek yoghurt with a little clear honey and season with salt and freshly ground black pepper. Sprinkle with plenty of chopped fresh mint and serve this tzatziki as a salad or a dip.

❋ Mix drained canned sweetcorn (corn) with drained chopped pimientos, a chopped tomato and a few chopped mushrooms. Dress with a vinaigrette dressing (see page 139).

❋ Toss cubes of feta cheese with sliced onions and tomatoes and dress with olive oil and black pepper.

❋ Combine walnuts and sliced apples with chopped celery and salad leaves and a light mayonnaise (see page 138).

❋ Sprinkle salads with chopped nuts, chopped fresh herbs or crumbled cheese.

Mayonnaise

Serves 4

	METRIC	IMPERIAL	AMERICAN
Egg	1	1	1
Egg yolk	1	1	1
Lemon juice	30 ml	2 tbsp	2 tbsp
White wine vinegar	15 ml	1 tbsp	1 tbsp
Mustard powder	2.5 ml	½ tsp	½ tsp
Salt and freshly ground black pepper			
Oil	375 ml	13 fl oz	1½ cups

1 Using a blender or whisk, blend together the egg, egg yolk, lemon juice, vinegar, mustard, salt and pepper. Add a little of the oil and whisk again.

2 Gradually add the remaining oil a little at a time, whisking or blending continuously until the mayonnaise thickens and emulsifies.

 Preparation time 10 minutes

Flavoured Mayonnaise

To make salad dressings or dips, add one of the following to 250 ml/8 fl oz/1 cup of mayonnaise:

* 30 ml/2 tbsp finely chopped fresh herbs such as parsley or tarragon;
* a few crushed garlic cloves;
* 15 ml/1 tbsp made mustard;

* 30 ml/2 tbsp finely chopped watercress, spring onions (scallions) or celery leaves;
* 15 ml/1 tbsp curry powder;
* 25 g/1 oz/¼ cup crumbled blue cheese;
* 45 ml/3 tbsp puréed beetroot (red beet).

Vinaigrette Dressing

Serves 4

	METRIC	IMPERIAL	AMERICAN
White wine vinegar	15 ml	1 tbsp	1 tbsp
Oil	45 ml	3 tbsp	3 tbsp
Mild mustard	5 ml	1 tsp	1 tsp
Salt and freshly ground black pepper			

Blend all the ingredients together well.

 Preparation time 5 minutes

Vinaigrette Variations

Choose from these flavours to add to a basic vinaigrette:

* 15 ml/1 tbsp chopped fresh herbs;
* 15 ml/1 tbsp chopped capers or gherkins (cornichons);
* 15 ml/1 tbsp chopped black or green olives.

Thousand Island Dressing

Serves 4

	METRIC	IMPERIAL	AMERICAN
Tomato purée (paste)	15 ml	1 tbsp	1 tbsp
Chopped red (bell) pepper	15 ml	1 tbsp	1 tbsp
Chopped green pepper	15 ml	1 tbsp	1 tbsp
Gherkin (cornichon), chopped	1	1	1
Hard-boiled (hard-cooked) egg, chopped	1	1	1
Mayonnaise (see page 138)	150 ml	¼ pt	⅔ cup

Blend the ingredients together well.

 Preparation time 5 minutes

Soy Dressing

Serves 4

	METRIC	IMPERIAL	AMERICAN
Soy sauce	60 ml	4 tbsp	4 tbsp
Lemon juice	15 ml	1 tbsp	1 tbsp
Oil	15 ml	1 tbsp	1 tbsp
Clear honey	20 ml	4 tsp	4 tsp
Ground ginger	2.5 ml	½ tsp	½ tsp
Water	60 ml	4 tbsp	4 tbsp

Blend all the ingredients together well.

 Preparation time 5 minutes

BARBECUE DESSERTS

A delicious dessert rounds off a meal nicely, especially if you are entertaining. Fruit is an excellent choice, not only because it barbecues well, but also because it offers a good taste counterpoint to a rich main course. Ice cream is always a summer favourite, especially with children, so keep some in the freezer and dress it up for the occasion.

~~~~~~~~~~~~~~~~

Melon and Grapes with Brie

Serves 6

	METRIC	IMPERIAL	AMERICAN
Cantaloupe melon	1	1	1
Honeydew melon	1	1	1
Watermelon	1/2	1/2	1/2
Seedless grapes	225 g	8 oz	1/2 lb
Fromage frais	90 ml	6 tbsp	6 tbsp
Brie cheese	100 g	4 oz	1/4 lb
Flaked almonds	50 g	2oz	1/2 cup

1 Cut the melons into wedges, discarding the seeds (pits) and peel, and arrange on serving plates. Arrange the grapes on top.

2 Place a spoonful of fromage frais at the side of each plate.

3 Cut the Brie into wedges and place on a piece of foil.

4 Barbecue for about 1 minute on each side until warm and slightly runny. Place on top of the fruits. Sprinkle with flaked almonds and serve at once.

Preparation time 10 minutes
Cooking time 2 minutes

Bananas Foster

Serves 4

	METRIC	IMPERIAL	AMERICAN
Butter or margarine, melted	45 ml	3 tbsp	3 tbsp
Light brown sugar	45 ml	3 tbsp	3 tbsp
Pinch of ground cinnamon			
Pinch of grated nutmeg			
Bananas, halved lengthways	4	4	4
To serve:			
Vanilla ice cream			
Chopped mixed nuts	60 ml	4 tbsp	4 tbsp

1 Mix the butter with the sugar, cinnamon and nutmeg. Brush the mixture over the bananas.

2 Place on a sheet of foil.

3 Barbecue for about 5 minutes until soft and browned.

4 Spoon into serving dishes and top with ice cream and nuts.

Preparation time 5 minutes
Cooking time 5 minutes

Gingered Melon

Serves 4

	METRIC	IMPERIAL	AMERICAN
Honeydew melon	1	1	1
Finely chopped crystallised (candied) ginger	15 ml	1 tbsp	1 tbsp
Finely chopped fresh root ginger	30 ml	2 tbsp	2 tbsp
Dry white wine	120 ml	4 fl oz	½ cup
Ground cinnamon	5 ml	1 tsp	1 tsp
Pinch of sugar			
Pinch of salt			

1 Peel the melon, then cut it into wedges.

2 Mix the crystallised and root ginger, the wine, cinnamon, sugar and salt in a pan and bring to the boil.

3 Add the melon wedges, remove from the heat, then leave to cool.

4 Drain the melon, reserving the liquid in the pan.

5 Boil the liquid until syrupy and reserve.

6 Barbecue the melon wedges for about 5 minutes until lightly browned, then serve with the sauce.

Preparation time 10 minutes plus cooling
Cooking time 10 minutes

Pears with Liqueur Cream

Serves 4

	METRIC	IMPERIAL	AMERICAN
Pears	4	4	4
Butter or margarine, melted	40 g	1½ oz	3 tbsp
Light brown sugar	100 g	4oz	½ cup
For the sauce:			
Fromage frais	225 g	8 oz	1 cup
Whipping cream, whipped	250 ml	8 fl oz	1 cup
Plain yoghurt	250 ml	8 fl oz	1 cup
Coffee liqueur	90 ml	6 tbsp	6 tbsp
Pinch of grated nutmeg			

1 Peel and core the pears and slice them thickly or cut them into wedges.

2 Mix the melted butter or margarine and half the sugar and brush over the pears.

3 Arrange on a piece of foil. Barbecue the pears for about 5 minutes until warm.

4 Blend together the fromage frais, cream, the remaining sugar, the yoghurt, liqueur and nutmeg.

5 Place the pears on serving plates and top with the liqueur cream.

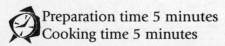
Preparation time 5 minutes
Cooking time 5 minutes

Orange Chestnut Kebabs

Serves 4

	METRIC	IMPERIAL	AMERICAN
Can of chestnuts, drained	225 g	8 oz	1 medium
Butter or margarine, melted	50 g	2 oz	¼ cup
Grated orange rind	10 ml	2 tsp	2 tsp
To serve:			
Light brown sugar	15 ml	1 tbsp	1 tbsp
Double (heavy) or whipping cream, whipped	150 ml	¼ pt	⅔ cup

1   Thread the chestnuts on to soaked wooden skewers.

2   Mix the butter with the orange rind and brush over the chestnuts.

3   Barbecue for about 5 minutes, turning frequently and brushing with the flavoured butter.

4   Sprinkle with sugar and serve with whipped cream.

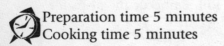
Preparation time 5 minutes
Cooking time 5 minutes

Cointreau Boats

Serves 4

	METRIC	IMPERIAL	AMERICAN
Bananas in their skins	4	4	4
Cointreau	30 ml	2 tbsp	2 tbsp
Demerara sugar	30 ml	2 tbsp	2 tbsp
Ground hazelnuts	30 ml	2 tbsp	2 tbsp

1 Barbecue the bananas in their skins for about 15 minutes until dark brown.

2 Carefully cut off a strip of skin about 1 cm/½ in wide along the length of the banana, sprinkle with Cointreau and leave for 1–2 minutes.

3 Sprinkle the banana flesh with sugar and hazelnuts and serve in the skins.

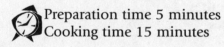
Preparation time 5 minutes
Cooking time 15 minutes

Chocolate Sandwiches

Especially popular with children, who can make up their own parcels while you are preparing the barbecue.

Serves 6

	METRIC	IMPERIAL	AMERICAN
Plain (semi-sweet) chocolate	225 g	8 oz	½ lb
Marshmallows	12	12	12
Digestive biscuits (Graham crackers)	12	12	12

1 Break the chocolate into squares. Arrange the chocolate and marshmallows on top of half the biscuits, then top with the other biscuits to make sandwiches. Wrap individually in foil.

2 Place the foil parcels on the barbecue for about 1–3 minutes. Serve at once.

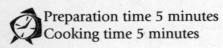
Preparation time 5 minutes
Cooking time 5 minutes

Barbecued Fruits

Barbecued fruits make a simple and tasty dessert.

* Arrange sliced fruits on a piece of foil, dot with butter and sprinkle lightly with sugar and a touch of cinnamon or freshly grated nutmeg. Sprinkle with a little rum or brandy, if you like. Seal the foil tightly then place on the barbecue for about 15 minutes. Try: thickly sliced peaches, pear halves, orange segments, pineapple rings, banana halves or sliced apples.

* Cinnamon and nutmeg are wonderful spices for sprinkling over fruit before cooking. Nutmeg is at its best if freshly grated as it loses its pungency very quickly.

* Don't ignore herbs with fruit. Those old favourites mint and rosemary go particularly well with fruits.

* Alternatively, try kebabs. Use firm fruits such as pineapple, apple, apricot, plums or kiwi fruit in different colours. Use just two or three fruits for each kebab, threading them alternately.

* Whether you are cooking whole or preparing as kebabs, soak fruits in a little dessert wine, red wine or your favourite liqueur for 30 minutes before barbecuing. Brush with melted butter or a little oil while they are cooking.

* You can barbecue bananas on the rack or even directly on the coals in their skins; they only take a few minutes to heat through and soften. Take great care when eating, though, as the whole thing gets very hot!

Fruit Salads

* A fruit salad is slightly more sophisticated. Select three or four different fruits with complementary colours and flavours. (Bananas tend to discolour and go very soft, so are best saved for hot dishes.) You can use what you have available, or try the following combinations: apples, melon, kiwi fruit and raspberries; pineapple, pears and mango; peaches, plums and apricots; oranges, grapes, pineapple and apples; blackberries, apples and redcurrants.

* Remove any cores or stones (pits) from fresh fruits. Whether you peel fruit is up to you. Some pears, for example, have a tasty skin, while others are rather coarse and might spoil the salad. To peel soft-skinned fruit, such as peaches, dip them in boiling water for about 20 seconds, then transfer to cold water and peel off the skin.

* Dice the fruit neatly in equal bite-sized pieces. Always have some lemon juice handy so that you can sprinkle it over apples, peaches or pears as soon as you cut them to prevent them from discolouring. Diced fruits will create their own juice; don't waste any while you are preparing the salad, simply add it to the bowl. If you feel that the salad needs a little more liquid, add a little orange or apple juice with a dash of sherry or brandy.

* Don't forget that you can also add canned fruits if you don't have enough fresh. Buy fruits in fruit juice or a light syrup for a fresh flavour; fruits in heavy syrup tend to be a little cloying.

* If you want to add a sugar syrup to the fruit salad, boil 275 g/10 oz/1¼ cups sugar with 600 ml/1 pt/2½ cups water and a squeeze of lemon juice until it is the consistency you prefer. Leave to cool before pouring

over the fruit. Alternatively use pure apple or orange juice as a 'base'.

* A few fresh or frozen strawberries – sliced if they are large – or raspberries can be scattered over the top for effect. Or, if you have just one kiwi fruit left, arrange it on top of the salad, rather than mixing it in.

* Garnish the fruit salad with a few fresh mint leaves and serve it on its own, or with a little cream or crème fraîche. Ice creams and sorbets also make good accompaniments.

Simple Fruit Ideas

A bowl of fresh fruit is the simplest and can be quite a spectacular dish. And there's nothing better than fruit to counter the sometimes rich flavours of the barbecue.

* There's no need for a vast range of fruits: two or three choices are plenty for an impromptu occasion, so simply arrange what you have attractively in a large bowl or on a platter.

* If you are buying specially, choose just three or four fruits which offer a contrast in texture and colour to make a stunning display for your table centre and a delicious end to the meal.

* Although we can now buy almost anything at almost any time of the year, choosing fruits in season usually means that you get the best value and the best quality.

* Buy one large water melon and cut it into thin crescents – deliciously refreshing if a little messy!

Ice Cream Ideas

✸ Dress up ordinary ice cream with a sprinkling of chopped nuts, sugar strands, chopped fresh or dried fruits or a drizzle of maple syrup, flower honey, your favourite ice cream sauce or fruit purée.

✸ Cut two flavours of ice cream – preferably in contrasting colours – into 1 cm/½ in cubes and serve on their own, or with similar-sized cubes of fruit.

✸ Layer scoops of ice cream, whipped cream, chopped nuts, toasted fresh breadcrumbs, soft fruits, fruit purée or thick sauce in sundae glasses and top with a swirl of whipped cream.

✸ Chop up your favourite chocolate-coated snack bar and melt with 60 ml/4 tbsp milk and a small knob of butter or margarine, stirring until smooth. Spoon over vanilla or chocolate ice cream.

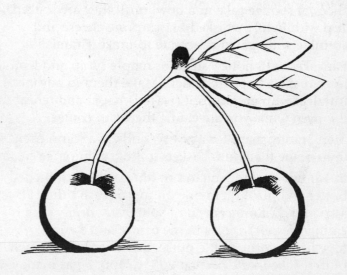

Other Dessert Ideas

* Sorbets and mousses make good barbecue desserts and can be bought or made in advance and kept in the fridge or freezer. Dress them up with some grated chocolate, grated orange rind, chopped nuts, fruit purée or fruit slices, depending on the flavour.

* Poach a few ready-to-eat dried apricot halves in apple juice with a slug of white wine or sherry for 10 minutes, then leave them to soak for as long as possible. Drain and serve topped with a spoonful of cranberry sauce and a swirl of cream.

* Cold desserts are always popular. Keep a frozen gâteau or special dessert such as a lemon tart in the freezer; it will only take a couple of hours to defrost when you decide to barbecue.

* Mix together equal quantities of strong black coffee and brandy or rum and spoon over sponge fingers or slices of sponge cake in a bowl until they are soaked. Top with lightly whisked Mascarpone cheese and sprinkle with grated chocolate to make Tiramisu.

* Pancakes with honey, sugar or maple syrup and lemon juice make a popular dessert. Make them in advance, interleaf with greaseproof (waxed) paper and reheat in the oven while you are eating the main course.

* Melt brandy snaps for a few seconds in a warm oven, then shape them into baskets to hold fruit or ice cream.

* Brush two or three squares of filo pastry with melted butter and place them one on top of each other. Place a spoonful of mincemeat or some very thinly sliced eating (dessert) apples in the centre and scrunch together to form a little purse. Brush with more melted butter. Bake in the oven at 200°C/400°F/gas mark 6 for about 10 minutes until crisp. Serve with cream.

* Dissolve 100 g/4 oz/½ cup caster (superfine) sugar over a very gentle heat until golden brown. Remove from the heat and add 60 ml/4 tbsp lemon juice and 750 ml/1¼ pts/3 cups water. Return to the heat, bring to the boil, then simmer for 3 minutes. Leave to cool, then stir in four sliced oranges and chill for as long as possible, preferably 4 hours.

* As a last-minute dessert, sandwich shortcake triangles together with whipped cream and soft fruit. Top with a swirl of cream and a little grated chocolate.

* Swirl a spoonful of colourful fruit purée, bottled chocolate sauce or sieved (strained) jam (conserve) into thick plain yoghurt for a simple but dramatic dessert.

* Purée a tub of Ricotta cheese with about half the quantity of drained canned peaches, then pile on slices of crusty bread or toast and sprinkle with light brown sugar.

INDEX